FINANCIAL PLANNING
for the
UTTERLY CONFUSED

Other titles by Joel Lerner

*Schaum's Outline of Introduction to Business Organization and
    Management*
Schaum's Outline of Bookkeeping and Accounting
Schaum's Outline of Introduction to Business (coauthor)
Schaum's Outline of Accounting I (coauthor)
Schaum's Outline of Accounting II (coauthor)
Schaum's Outline of Intermediate Accounting I (coauthor)
Schaum's Outline of Business Mathematics (coauthor)
Introduction to Business: A Contemporary Reader (editor)
Readings in Business Organization and Management (editor)

$·$·$ FINANCIAL PLANNING for the UTTERLY CONFUSED

Joel Lerner

McGraw-Hill Book Company

New York   St. Louis   San Francisco   Auckland   Bogotá
Guatemala   Hamburg   Johannesburg   Lisbon   London
Madrid   Mexico   Montreal   New Delhi   Panama   Paris
San Juan   São Paulo   Singapore   Sydney   Tokyo   Toronto

1 2 3 4 5 6 7 8 9 FGRFGR 8 7 6 5

ISBN 0-07-037224-1

LIBRARY OF CONGRESS CATALOGING-IN-PUBLICATION DATA

Lerner, Joel J.
    Financial planning for the utterly confused.

    1. Finance, Personal—United States.   2. Investments-
United States.   I. Title.
HG179.L45   1985   332.024   85-19823
ISBN 0-07-037224-1

BOOK DESIGN BY PATRICE FODERO

To the members of the middle class—
who pay for the tax shelters of the rich
as well as the food stamps of the poor

Contents

••

Introduction   ix

PART ONE   Financial Instruments from A to Z   **1**

Annuities   3
Certificates of Deposit   9
Condominiums and Co-ops   14
Corporate Bonds   22
Gold, Silver, and Diamonds   31
Government-Insured Mortgages (Ginnie Maes)   40
The Individual Retirement Account   47
The Keogh Plan   57
Life Insurance   60
Money Market Funds   65
Mortgages   71
Municipal Bonds   77
Municipal Bond Trusts and Funds   86
Mutual Funds   91
Oil and Gas Shelters   98
Public Utilities   102
Real Estate   107
The Salary Reduction Plan: 401(k) Plan   113
Stocks   116
Stock Options and Commodity Futures   133
Treasury Bills, Notes, and Bonds   141
U.S. Savings Bonds   147
Zero Coupon Bonds   153

PART TWO   Knowing Your Estate   **159**

Divorce and Taxes   161
Early Retirement   165
Federal Deposit Insurance   168
Financial Planning for Women   171
Joint Ownership   176
Lump-Sum Distributions   179
The Safe-Deposit Box   182
Taxation of Social Security   184
Trusts   188
Wills   192

PART THREE   A Glossary of Financial Terms   197

Introduction

I am a teacher, not a stockbroker, bank executive, or insurance salesperson. My specialty isn't fancy jargon, hucksterism, or statistics. Rather, it's explaining financial and economic matters to ordinary people in plain English. That's what *Financial Planning for the Utterly Confused* is all about.

The largest portion of this book consists of an easy-to-read, alphabetically arranged listing of the various kinds of investments—**financial instruments,** as they are called—which the typical middle-income investor is likely to be interested in. You won't find tips on high-flying stocks that promise to help you double your money overnight. As you already know, no one can make such promises with any certainty. What you will find here is an honest appraisal of the advantages, disadvantages, costs, and benefits of each type of financial instrument. Based on this information, you'll be able to make a sound decision as to whether or not a particular investment is right for you.

As you'll learn, the single most important factor in deciding on the best investments for you is the level of risk you can afford to take. Thus the first step in formulating your investment plan is a careful self-examination. How much money do you have to invest? How great will your financial needs be for the foreseeable future? How much of your capital can you realistically afford to risk losing? And how great a degree of risk can you and your family handle psychologically? Each of these factors will have a bearing on the amount of risk tolerance you can bring to your investment decisions.

If you must put your money only into investments with virtually no risk, then government obligations such as U.S. Treasury bills, notes, or bonds are probably your best choice. (You'll read about these instruments in Part One.) If your finances can tolerate a higher degree of risk in the interest of a potentially greater gain, then a wider range of alternatives may be appropriate. A series of new guidelines comes into play:

1. Don't invest in an instrument in which you could lose more than potentially gain. This factor is sometimes referred to as **risk/reward balance.**
2. Diversify your holdings. Spread your investment dollars among a variety of instruments, thereby minimizing the risk potential.
3. When investments fail to perform up to your expectations, sell them. "Cutting your losses" is the only sure way to prevent minor setbacks from turning into financial nightmares. Remember that bulls can make money, bears can make money, but pigs get slaughtered.

Just how these general principles apply to different types of investments will become clear as you read through Part One.

Part Two covers a variety of special financial topics of interest to particular groups of people or to investors at a particular stage in their lives. You're sure to find some subjects of concern to you or your family in these pages.

Part Three is a glossary of terms commonly used in the financial world. You'll find it a handy reference tool when reading the money-managing columns in your daily newspaper or your favorite magazine. And it should help you penetrate some of the verbal fog generated by brokers, bankers, and salespeople.

My hope is that *Financial Planning for the Utterly Confused* will be a valuable tool for the millions of Americans who need help in managing their small- to medium-sized investment plans. The information in this book can be for you the first building block in the creation of a secure and comfortable financial future.

Joel Lerner

PART ONE

••

Financial Instruments
from A to Z

Annuities

••

*A tax-saving way of providing yourself with retirement income you
know you'll never outlive*

When you retire, you'll want to be able to live comfortably
for life on the income from your investments. However,
thanks to modern medicine, many people run the risk of
outliving their investment income. One way of avoiding
this risk is by establishing an *annuity.*

An annuity can be considered the opposite of a traditional insurance policy. When you buy insurance, you
agree to pay annual premiums to an insurance company.
In return, the company will pay the face value of the policy in a lump sum to your beneficiaries when you die. By
contrast, when you buy an annuity, you pay the company a
sum of money and, in return, receive a monthly income
for as long as you live. Naturally, the longer you live, the
more money you'll receive. You might say that life insurance protects you against financial loss as a result of dying
too soon, while an annuity protects you against financial
loss as a result of living too long.

There are several different types of annuities. They
can be categorized according to three main characteristics:

1. **Premiums.** An annuity may be purchased either through a single lump-sum premium or through annual premium payments. If you happen to have a large sum of money to invest at one time—for example, from an inheritance or from withdrawal of funds from a pension fund—you may want to purchase an annuity with a lump-sum payment. Once you've made the initial investment, no further contributions are required. Under an annual payment plan, contributions are made each year for a predetermined period.

2. **Payment Return.** An annuity may provide for either *immediate* return to the investor or *deferred* return. An immediate annuity is purchased at the time you want to start receiving income, and it requires a single lump-sum premium. The insurance company begins sending you monthly checks right away. One caution: When you buy an immediate annuity, you forfeit all liquidity; that is, you can't change your mind and withdraw your money from the investment. A deferred annuity, on the other hand, is purchased at some time prior to the time when income is needed. The waiting period is called the *deferral period*. During the deferral period, which may be very short or may last up to 40 years, your investment earns interest tax-free. You can also withdraw your money from the annuity during that time, although you may lose some of your interest when you do.

3. **Return on Investment.** Annuities may be classified as either *fixed-dollar* or *variable*. Fixed-dollar annuities are the more traditional kind. They guarantee

you a certain minimum interest rate. The actual rate you'll receive is fixed for only a few months or years, but there is a minimum rate below which your return cannot drop. Insurance companies usually invest fixed-dollar annuity funds in highly secure investments, such as government bonds. With a fixed-dollar annuity, you'll know that your principal is safe and that you'll receive at least a specified minimum income.

Variable annuities, on the other hand, are usually invested in more risky, but potentially more lucrative, investments, such as common stock and money market instruments. Therefore, variable annuities are affected by inflation, economic conditions, and the strength of particular investments. The amount of interest your money earns, and therefore the size of the payments you'll receive, will vary according to the success of the insurance company's investments. In addition, your principal is not untouchable. A stock market disaster could wipe out all or part of your investment. So you may earn more with a variable annuity, but the risk is greater.

As we've explained, with an annuity, the longer you live, the greater return you can expect to earn. This means, of course, that if you die early, you may never earn back the amount you originally paid for the annuity. Some kinds of annuities have built-in provisions to minimize this risk. Some annuities contain "years certain" provisions, which guarantee payments for a specified period—usually 10 to 20 years—even if you die. Your beneficiary receives the benefits in such a case. Other annuities contain a *refund* provision, which specifies that the amount of your total investment will be refunded to your beneficiary in the event you die before having received that amount in payments. Finally, a *joint and survivor* annuity guarantees payments to either of two parties, such as a husband and wife, as long as either of them lives. Naturally, any of these special provisions will add to the cost of an annuity.

Annuities provide certain income tax benefits that are of special benefit to middle-income investors. You'll find that your assets accumulate more quickly than with most other investments, because the interest you earn is not subject to income tax until you begin to withdraw it. In effect, you'll be earning interest on the initial investment, on the interest itself (because of compounding), and on the money you *don't* have to pay the government.

There's another tax benefit to consider. With an annuity, you can transfer your investment from one account to another without incurring any tax liability on the money you've gained. Here's what we mean: Suppose you purchased a $20,000 tax-deferred annuity invested in common stock. After several years, the value of the annuity might have increased to $30,000. If you wanted to, you could transfer that $30,000 to any other annuity account (perhaps to take advantage of some new investment opportunity) without any tax liability. With other investment vehicles, this isn't possible. Transferring the $30,000 investment from one account to another would make you immediately subject to tax on the $10,000 increase in the value of the investment.

Of special interest to the middle-income investor is the **tax-deferred annuity.** As the name implies, money you invest in a tax-deferred annuity is exempt from federal income tax. You can deduct the amount of your investment from your income immediately, thereby reducing your tax bill. You'll have to pay taxes on the money you invest only later, when the annuity payments begin. If you're using the annuity as a retirement fund, you'll be in a lower tax bracket then, so the tax bite will be less.

Not all investors are eligible to buy a tax-deferred annuity. Those employed by public schools, many hospitals, or other kinds of nonprofit institutions are among those eligible. Check with your employer. If you're eligible to invest in one, a tax-deferred annuity can be an excellent buy.

You can buy a lump-sum annuity from an insurance company or through an investment broker for as little as $5000. The average lump-sum annuity costs between $20,000 and $30,000. Be sure to ask your agent or broker about sales charges before you buy. These charges, known as *front-end loads,* may run as high as 15 percent of your investment.

Most companies charge annual administrative fees which further reduce your income. These fees vary, but they average around 1.5 percent of the amount invested. Find out the amount of the fee before you invest, and compare the rates charged by several companies.

Also note that most companies impose a surrender charge if you cash in your annuity early. The size of this penalty will vary from company to company. Typically, you may be charged a penalty of 7 percent of your investment if you withdraw it during the first year, 6 percent during the second year, 5 percent during the third year, and so on. From the eighth year on, no penalty is charged. Ask about surrender charges before deciding on where to invest in an annuity.

How safe is an annuity investment? Generally speaking, as safe as the company that issues it. The insurance company guarantees the value of your investment and is required to maintain cash reserves to cover withdrawals.

In many states, additional protection exists. New York State, for example, has set up a guarantee fund from which the owner of an annuity will be reimbursed if the issuer of the annuity is unable to pay. Find out whether your state has such a fund; 21 of the 50 do not.

Traditionally, annuities have not paid outstanding rates of return. You may find that other forms of investment will provide you with a greater retirement income. Do some comparison shopping before you invest; annuities are not for everyone. However, annuities—especially tax-deferred annuities—have certain distinct advantages for investors in the 30 to 50 percent tax brackets. The most important benefit, of course, lies in the fact that annuity income is guaranteed for life, no matter how long you live. It's pretty comforting to retire with an income that you know you can never outlive.

Certificates of Deposit

••

One of the most versatile investment options available, offering both high yields and flexible terms—but you'll find that it really pays to shop around before you buy

At one time, you needed $100,000 or more to invest in a bank *certificate of deposit.* This restriction had been established by the Federal Reserve Board in order to protect savings banks, savings and loan institutions, and credit unions from competition with commercial banks. The fear was that if commercial banks could issue high-yielding certificates of deposit in small denominations, small savers would withdraw their funds from low-yielding passbook savings accounts in order to buy the certificates. This, in turn, would hurt the savings banks, most of whose holdings were tied up in low-yielding, long-term mortgages. In effect, the Federal Reserve sought to protect the banks at the expense of small savers.

All this changed after 1972, when the first money market mutual fund offered its shares for sale for as little as $1000. Money market funds, which paid rates comparable to those offered on bank certificates of deposit, quickly became a favorite investment for small savers. The savings banks began to lose customers. As a result, the banks themselves demanded that the rules be changed so as to allow them to compete with the money market funds. Thus was born the certificate of deposit (**CD**) for the small investor.

Today, most federal restrictions governing insured term deposits in banks have been lifted. Banks are free to compete with one another in setting terms for their own CDs. You can now buy a high-yielding CD for as little as $1000 from a savings and loan, a savings bank, a credit union, a commercial bank, or a broker. The competition between these various suppliers tends to keep rates high. For the small saver, the revolution of the 1970s and 1980s has been highly beneficial.

The concept of the CD is simple. It is a savings instrument issued by a financial institution which pays you high interest at a guaranteed rate for a specified term. The amount you invest in a CD is insured by the federal government for up to $100,000; so a CD is a safe investment.

There are two primary considerations in planning your investment in a CD: (1) the term of the investment and (2) the rate of return.

Term: The most popular type of CD is the 6-month certificate, but CDs are available with maturities ranging from 7 days up to 10 years. During the term of your CD, the money you've invested is relatively costly to liquidate (illiquid). If an emergency arises which requires you to withdraw your money before maturity, you'll be penalized for it. Thus you'll want to consider carefully when you're likely to need the money before you invest in a CD. If a college tuition bill is due to be paid in 1 year and 3 months, you know that you'll want a certificate which matures at that time.

One rule to remember: The longer the term of the certificate, the higher the rate of return. So it's generally to your advantage to invest in the longest-term CD you can reasonably choose. A second rule is this: The longer the term of the certificate, the lower the minimum investment required. So depending on the amount of money you have to invest, you may face some limitations on the term of the CDs available to you.

Rate of Return: The interest paid on a CD will vary not only according to the term of the certificate but also from time to time, as interest rates fluctuate, as well as from bank to bank. Don't buy your CD at the first bank you visit; the competing bank across the street may well be offering half a point more. Shop around.

Ask about how the bank credits the interest earned to your account. The more frequently interest is credited, the better for you, since each time your account grows through an interest payment, the amount of money you have working for you grows as well. Over the term of a CD, the differences among accounts can be substantial. Here's an example. A $10,000 deposit at a rate of 8.5 percent interest will earn $850 if there is no compounding. If interest is credited to the account quarterly, the amount earned rises to $877. With monthly compounding, the interest earned is $883, and with daily compounding, $900. So do investigate these policies. If you find a bank that compounds your interest daily, you may want to do your investing there.

In their advertising, banks will sometimes reflect their compounding policies by listing a true rate of return along with the nominal rate for a given CD.

Thus a CD with a nominal rate of 8.05 percent may pay a true rate, with compounding, of 8.32 percent. Use the true rates, if available, for comparison purposes.

Some other points to compare when shopping for the best deal on a CD:

- Ask about variable-rate CDs. These rates are usually based on the current rates on Treasury bills issued by the federal government. They may be higher or lower than the rates paid on fixed-rate CDs, depending on financial conditions.

- Ask whether you can increase the size of your investment after the original purchase of your CD. This can be advantageous if you expect more funds to be available shortly (and if you expect interest rates to decline in the future).

- Ask whether the bank offers bonuses of any kind upon purchase of a CD. Due to competitive pressures, some banks offer $25 or $50 bonuses at the time of your investment. Others offer gifts, such as small appliances, or special services, such as no-fee credit card accounts or free checking.

- Don't forget that since 1982 brokers have also been able to offer CDs. The certificates sold by brokers are units, usually in denominations of $1000 or more, of larger certificates issued by savings institutions. Broker-sold CDs have one major advantage over those purchased directly from banks. Brokers are not required to charge a penalty on early withdrawal of invested funds. If you wish, you can sell your CD back to the broker at the current market rate without incurring any penalty.

In addition, when considering buying a CD, compare them to such similar investment instruments as Treasury notes. On the one hand, a Treasury note pays interest which is free of state and local taxes, unlike the CD whose earnings are fully taxable. The Treasury note can also be sold, through a broker, before reaching maturity without involving a penalty. On the other hand, the market value of a long-term Treasury note can decline drastically if interest rates rise. With a CD, a sharp increase in interest rates can be much less painful. The worst that can happen is a partial loss of interest, in the event you decide to withdraw your investment before maturity in order to take advantage of the new higher rates available. The more lucrative investment into which you shift your funds will probably more than make up for that loss. So look carefully at your alternatives before making a decision.

Given all these factors, it seems safe to say that the bank CD—with its high degree of safety, relatively high rate of return, and flexibility as to term—will remain a deservedly popular investment choice for the foreseeable future.

Condominiums and Co-ops

••

Two ways of obtaining some of the financial benefits of home ownership while enjoying the convenience of apartment dwelling

If you live in a rented apartment, you probably realize that owning your own home would provide you with some important financial advantages. For one thing, there are substantial tax benefits associated with mortgage interest and property tax payments. For another, the equity you build up as you pay for your home will probably represent a sizable nest egg by the time you're ready to sell. And with the traditionally strong upward trend in real estate prices, you'll probably find that the value of your home has increased substantially during your period of ownership.

But what if you can't afford to buy your own home? What if you prefer to live in an apartment, where the building is maintained and repaired by others with a minimum of headaches for you? Or what if there are few or no affordable homes in the areas you want to live in? For any or all of these reasons, you may want to consider buying a condominium or cooperative apartment as an alternative to home ownership.

A *condominium,* or condo, is an arrangement in which

you own your own dwelling unit, usually an apartment but sometimes an individual house, row house, duplex, or other unit. You also own a share in the common properties used by all the owners in a particular building or complex, including the land, the lobby, the heating and electrical system, and the parking lots as well as any community facilities, such as a golf course, recreation hall, or swimming pool. You must pay a monthly maintenance fee to the developer of the condominium, which covers your share of the operating costs. In addition, you must pay your own property taxes and any mortgage you need to buy the apartment, just as most homeowners do.

Since you are the owner of your own condominium unit, the finances of condominium ownership resemble those of buying a house. You must arrange for your own financing, generally by taking out a mortgage from a bank or other financial institution. (Mortgage money for condominiums is usually readily available, sometimes at interest rates slightly lower than those charged for home mortgages.) The portion of your mortgage payments devoted to interest payment is deductible from your income for purposes of federal taxation—a substantial benefit for condominium owners. Your property tax payments, too, are deductible from your federal income tax. And since you own your condominium unit, you can sell it when you like to whomever you wish. If the value of the property has grown, you may walk away with a tidy profit.

As you can see, condominium ownership can confer some important benefits. Here are some of the other advantages of owning a condo unit:

- It usually costs less to buy a condominium than to buy a private home, and, as we've already mentioned, condo financing is often easier to arrange.

- Condominium projects are professionally maintained, which can alleviate much of the anxiety of owning your own home. This can be especially important for the elderly, who may want to escape chores, such as painting, shoveling snow, trimming hedges, and so on.
- Safety and security are usually tighter in a multiple dwelling, such as a condo apartment complex, than in an isolated private home—another important consideration for older people in particular.
- Finally, the sharing of costs among a large group of owners permits luxuries individual homeowners usually can't afford—swimming pools, tennis courts, clubhouses, and the like.

This is not to say that condo ownership is without drawbacks or pitfalls. Here are some cautionary notes to consider before making a condo purchase:

- When investigating a particular condominium project, check the quality and condition of the property carefully. Make sure the plumbing, electrical, and heating systems are in good working order. The developer should be willing to certify the condition of the structure. If the condominium is in a newly built development, don't rely on assurances that special facilities, like a pool or golf course, will "soon be available." If these amenities aren't in place and operating when you buy, you may never see them.
- When you own a condo, all decisions concerning the common properties of the condominium project are made by a management committee and ratified by a vote of the individual owners. The weight of your vote depends on the size of your unit: the bigger your apartment, the more votes you'll have. Nonetheless, the wishes of the majority of owners will

normally prevail. Can this become a problem? Yes, if decisions are made which affect living conditions at the condo in ways you don't approve.

- The maintenance fee you pay is not permanently fixed. It may increase due to ordinary price inflation. It may also have to be boosted if the maintenance budget initially set by the developer was unrealistically low. This is something to consider carefully before buying.

- When you wish to sell your condo, you don't need the permission of the management committee. However, the committee often has the right of first refusal on your property, and so may require early notification of your intention to sell.

Condo ownership can be ideal for many people. But make sure you understand the terms of the arrangement before you get involved. See the maintenance fees spelled out, read the rules and restrictions carefully, and have the condition of the property checked out thoroughly. Above all, be sure you're dealing with an established, reputable developer. Talk to friends, call the local Better Business Bureau, and ask at your bank. If anything you hear makes you doubt the reliability of the seller, back off.

A *cooperative,* or co-op, differs from a condominium in several ways. When you buy a co-op, you buy a share or a number of shares in the corporation that owns and manages the land and the buildings. These shares entitle you to occupy a particular apartment for a specified term. However, you do not own the apartment, as you would when buying a condo. As a co-op owner, you must pay a monthly maintenance fee, which includes not only your share of the cost of maintaining the building and grounds (like the condo maintenance fee) but also your share of the mortgage costs and taxes *on the entire property,* which are paid by the corporation as a whole. In addition, of course, you may have to make payments on the mortgage loan you took out to purchase your shares in the co-op.

Note that you can deduct from your federal income taxes the portion of your monthly maintenance fee which goes to pay for interest on the corporate mortgage and property taxes. If you take out a mortgage of your own, those interest costs are deductible as well.

There are other differences between a condo and a co-op. When decisions affecting the management of the development must be made, condo owners have voting power weighted according to the size of the units they own. A co-op owner has a single vote, regardless of the size of the apartment he or she may own. A condo owner may sell the unit to anyone (although the management usually has the right of first refusal). By contrast, the corporation which manages the co-op has complete control over the buying and selling of apartments. You may be required to sell your apartment only to the corporation; you will certainly have to obtain permission before you can sell it to anyone else. And the corporation will probably also have to approve any major alterations you wish to make in your apartment. However, as with a condo, any appreciation in the value of your co-op apartment during your period of ownership will benefit you when the time comes to sell.

The strict control over the property held by a co-op's management can be both an advantage and a disadvantage to the individual owner. On the one hand, it restricts your freedom to do as you like with the apartment. On the other hand, as a voting shareholder in the corporation, you may like the idea that the corporation can limit and control the uses to which the property is put and, to some extent, the people who move in. In fact, this feature of the co-op has been used by many wealthy people as a way of preventing those whom they considered "undesirable" from becoming their neighbors. If you're a typical middle-income person, this approach will probably not have much appeal to you.

There is one more important difference between condo and co-op ownership. When you buy shares in a co-op, you are investing in a corporation and, in effect, becoming business partners with the other co-op owners. This means that, like a shareholder in any corporation, you can be held responsible for the solvency of the enterprise. If not enough people sign up to become co-op shareholders, the maintenance fees charged to those who have already purchased their shares must go up to pay the difference. And if other co-op owners default on their maintenance payments, you will have to help make up the difference. Therefore, the reliability of those buying shares in the co-op should be an important consideration in deciding whether or not to get involved.

On balance, the condominium is probably a more favorable choice for most people than the co-op. However, if you're an apartment renter, you may find one day that the owner of your building has decided to "go co-op," that is, to attempt to convert the building from rentals to co-ops, with the former owner as the manager of the newly formed corporation. If this happens, you will, of course, be faced with the decision as to whether or not you wish to purchase shares in the co-op. If you decide that you do, based on your financial situation and how well you like your apartment, fine. If for some reason you prefer not to join the co-op, you should be aware of the rights you have as a renter in a building going co-op. These rights will vary from one state and city to another, due to local laws. The discussion that follows is based on current New York City laws. You will have to investigate the current legal situation in your own area to determine how the laws there may differ.

The owner who wishes to convert his or her building into a co-op must offer tenants either an *eviction* or a *non-eviction* conversion plan. With an eviction plan, which must first be approved by the state attorney general, the owner must convince 51 percent of the building's current occupants to become shareholders in the co-op. Once this percentage is reached, the co-op plan goes into effect. Those who choose not to purchase shares in the co-op can be evicted under this plan. However, if they choose, they have the right to remain in the building as renters for up to 3 years before they can be forced to leave. An exception is made for senior citizens and the handicapped, who are not subject to eviction at any time. They are also protected as renters, by rent stabilization or rent control as long as their apartments were so covered before the conversion.

Under a non-eviction plan, tenants who choose not to enter into a co-op agreement can remain in their apartments as renters under the same terms and conditions that existed before the building went co-op.

Again, these rules may vary, depending on where you live. If you're confronted with a co-op conversion plan in the building you live in, you and your fellow tenants may want to retain a real estate attorney to advise you in more detail about your rights and guide you through the conversion process.

As you can see, either a condominium or a co-op can be a worthwhile investment. Both provide tax advantages that renting cannot offer, and with both arrangements you own a property (either the actual dwelling unit or a share in the co-op) which has a good chance of growing in value while you use it. Therefore, if you're currently renting the home in which you live and buying a house is either impractical or just not your cup of tea, look into the local condo and co-op markets. Both are options well worth considering.

Corporate Bonds

● ●

A relatively safe, high-yielding investment that is growing in popularity among small investors—but one that requires knowledge, judgment, and a cool head

Although bonds have become popular with many investors, they are still widely misunderstood. There are many kinds of bonds, and investing in them wisely can be a complex, challenging task. However, the rewards are often great, and bonds are an option well worth investigating for the middle-class investor.

A *bond* is a form of debt issued by a government or a corporation. In exchange for a sum of money lent by the buyer of the bond, the issuer of the bond promises to pay a specific amount of interest at stated intervals for a specific period of time. At the end of the repayment period (that is, at maturity), the issuer repays the amount of money borrowed.

You can read about the bonds issued by the federal government elsewhere in this book. In this section, we'll discuss the special characteristics of corporate bonds—those issued by corporations.

The holder of a corporate bond is a creditor of the corporation which issues the bond, not a part owner like a stockholder. Therefore, if the corporation's profits increase during the term of the bond, the bondholder will not benefit; the amount of interest he or she receives is fixed at the time the bond is purchased. On the other hand, the bondholder's investment is safer than that of the stockholder. Interest on bonds is paid out before dividends are distributed to stockholders. Furthermore, if the corporation goes bankrupt, the claims of bondholders take precedence over those of stockholders.

Newly issued corporate bonds are usually sold by a brokerage firm, which acts as underwriter of the issue. The underwriter receives the bonds from the issuing corporation and guarantees the corporation a specified level of sales. The underwriter then sells the bonds to the public. This is known as the *primary* bond market.

There is also a *secondary* bond market. It, too, operates through brokerage firms. The secondary market deals in previously issued bonds, which, as you'll see, may have either increased or decreased in value since their initial offering.

Some bonds are issued with property (such as land, buildings, machinery, or other equipment) as collateral against the loan, just as you might offer collateral to a bank in exchange for a personal loan. These bonds are known as *secured bonds*. Bonds not secured by collateral are called **debentures.** The value of a debenture is guaranteed by the good faith of the corporation. A debenture issued by a strong corporation can be a highly secure investment.

All bonds bear both a face value and a maturity date. The face value is the amount you normally must spend to buy the bond when it is issued; it represents the amount of money you are lending the issuing corporation. The maturity date is when the face value of the bond must be repaid. Thus a 20-year bond issued in 1986 must be repaid in full in 2006.

Interest on corporate bonds is usually paid in one of two ways. *Coupon bonds,* also called *bearer bonds,* have interest coupons attached to them. You clip the coupons as they become due and present them for payment of interest. Your name usually doesn't appear on a coupon bond; it is a negotiable instrument, and anyone who clips the coupons can claim the interest due. However, this type of bond is no longer issued. By contrast, a *registered bond* bears its owner's name and can be transferred from one owner to another only by the endorsement of the registered owner. Interest on a registered bond is paid through the mail by check.

Corporate bonds are usually issued in denominations of $1000. After issue, however, their prices vary. A bond's **par value** is $1000, and its value at any given time is quoted as a percentage of par. Thus a bond quoted at 100 is selling at 100 percent of par, or $1000. If the price is quoted at 95, it is selling at 95 percent of par; you could buy such a bond for $950. This is known as a *discounted bond.* A *premium bond* is one which sells at a price higher than par. A bond with a quoted price of 102, for example, will cost $1020, which is 102 percent of par.

Why does the price of a corporate bond fluctuate? This is because of the fixed rate paid by the bond. As the current market interest rate increases, the relative value of the fixed rate paid by a bond decreases and so does the price of the bond. When the current market interest rate decreases, the fixed rate paid by the bond becomes increasingly attractive, and the value of the bond goes up as a result.

There are many variations in the types of bonds issued by corporations. You should understand some of the most important ones.

A bond may be issued with a *callability* or *redeemability* clause. A callable bond may be redeemed by the issuing corporation prior to the maturity date; that is, the corporation may, at its option, call in the bonds early and repay them at that time (though usually at a premium over their face value). The corporation is likely to exercise this option when market interest rates have fallen below those in effect at the time the bond was issued. If new market conditions call for interest rates of 10 percent, why should a corporation continue to pay 12 or 14 percent on its previously issued bonds? As you can see, callability is a drawback for the investor, since it prevents you from locking in high interest rates. For this reason, callable bonds usually pay a higher interest rate than comparable non-callable bonds.

Recently, some corporations have begun to offer protection for a specified period against the possibility of a bond's being called. This "call protection" usually runs 5 to 10 years, and it guarantees the bondholder a specific interest rate for at least a minimum number of years. Always check the call provision in any bond contract you are considering.

Some corporations issue *convertible bonds,* which may be exchanged for shares of the corporation's common stock at the option of the bondholder. This can allow you to participate in a greater-than-expected growth in the profits and value of the corporation. Convertible bonds thus combine the stability and safety of bonds with the growth opportunity of common stock. As usual, however, there's no free lunch: You must ordinarily sacrifice about 1 percentage point in interest yield in exchange for the convertibility feature,

There are two principal factors to weigh in considering the purchase of a particular corporate bond: (1) the yield offered by the bond and (2) the safety of the investment. Let's consider each of these factors in some detail.

Yield: As applied to bonds, the very term "yield" can be confusing. There are several types of yields associated with bonds.

The *coupon yield,* or *coupon rate,* is the interest rate stated on the bond itself.

The *actual yield* is the ratio of return that the coupon yield actually produces when the cost of the bond is taken into account. If you purchase the bond above par, the actual yield is lower than the coupon yield; if you purchase the bond below par, the actual yield is higher. For example, a $1000 bond with an 8 percent coupon rate bought at 82 (for a cost of $820) would produce an actual yield of 9.7 percent (since the $80 annual interest payment amounts to 9.7 percent of the $820 cost of the bond, that is, $80 divided by $820). The same bond bought at 104 (for a cost of $1040) would actually yield only 7.7 percent.

The *current yield* is the actual yield based on the closing price of the bond on the bond market for a given day. When the price of the bond declines, the current yield increases; when the price of the bond increases, the current yield declines.

Finally, *yield to maturity* represents the total rate of return if the bond is held to maturity, taking into consideration the purchase price of the bond, the interest paid, and the redemption price. Any broker can refer to a standard reference book which contains yield to maturity figures for almost any conceivable bond.

Naturally, all things being equal, the higher the yield on a particular bond, the better buy that bond is likely to be. But all things are not always equal. Bonds also differ in their degree of safety. That brings us to the second dominant consideration in choosing a bond for purchase.

Safety: The degree of risk associated with the purchase of a particular bond depends on the strength of the issuing corporation. Of course, it's not easy for the average middle-income investor to analyze the performance of all the many bond-issuing corporations. For a full examination, it would be necessary to study the company's financial statements, its earnings projections, the track record of management, prospects for the industry, and many other factors.

Fortunately, you don't need to do all this research yourself. There are special advisory services which have assumed the task of analyzing and rating the safety of corporate bonds. These ratings can be obtained from reference books readily obtained at your public library or from any brokerage house.

The two best-known ratings services are Moody's and Standard & Poor's (S&P). They rate bonds along two slightly differing scales. Starting with the highest-rated bonds, the two scales are as follows:

Moody's: Aaa, Aa, A, Baa, Ba, B, Caa, Ca, C

S&P: AAA, AA, A, BBB, BB, B, CCC, CC, C

The most risk-free bonds—those issued by large, stable corporations showing excellent future earnings projections—are rated Aaa or AAA. Bonds rated AA or A are issued by firms whose ability to pay interest and principal is quite strong, but the safety of these bonds is somewhat more vulnerable to changes in economic conditions.

As you move toward the lower end of the rating scale, yields are likely to be higher; the lower-rated firms must offer higher interest rates to induce investors to accept the greater degree of risk. The bonds on the lowest rungs of the ladder are sometimes called "junk bonds." These bonds, constituting about 10 percent of the total bond market, have ratings of BB or lower and usually pay yields about 3 percentage points higher than A-rated bonds. They received their disparaging nickname in the late 1920s and early 1930s, when the Great Depression led to numerous defaults by bond issuers. Yet the risk of default even on junk bonds is surprisingly low. Since the depression, the historic default rate is below 1 percent.

Most brokers will quote the standard bond ratings along with prices and yields when you inquire about possible investments. For maximum safety, you'll probably want to stick to bonds in the A and higher categories. The only exception would be if you want to choose a low-rated, high-yielding bond on a speculative basis. If you do, make sure that the amount you risk in this way is no greater than you can afford to lose. Greed—especially for the ill-informed investor—can lead to devastating mistakes.

If you're interested in getting into the bond market, you should know how to read the bond quotations which appear on the business page of your daily newspaper. These are a good basic source of information about currently available bonds. Figure 1 provides a sample bond listing as it might appear in the newspaper. You'll find an explanation of the information each column provides below the sample listing.

At any given time, there are approximately 5000 different bonds available from U.S. corporations on either the New York or American exchange. Keeping up with all these issues is a formidable task, which no typical middle-class investor can reasonably handle. Therefore, you may want to consider investing in a mutual fund which specializes in corporate bonds. Such funds, which are available through major brokerage houses, offer several advantages. You can buy a share in a bond fund for as little as

Issue	Description	Current Yield	Volume	High	Low	Last	Change
ABC	8¾ 96	9.8	28	90½	88	89	+1½

Issue: The abbreviated name of the corporation issuing the bond; in this case, ABC.

Description: A description of the bond. This bond has a coupon yield of 8¾ percent and matures in 1996.

Current Yield: The annual interest on a $1000 bond divided by today's closing price for the bond. In this case, 8¾ percent of $1000 ($87.50) divided by $890 = 9.8 percent.

Volume: The number of $1000 bonds traded that day.

High: The highest price of the day; in this case, 90½ percent of par, or $905 for a $1000 bond.

Low: The lowest price of the day; in this case, 88 percent of par, or $880 for a $1000 bond.

Last: The day's closing price; in this case, 89 percent of par, or $890 for a $1000 bond.

Change: The difference between today's closing price and yesterday's. Since today's closing price of $890 is 1½ points higher than yesterday's, yesterday's closing price must have been $875.

Figure 1. Sample Corporate Bond Listing

$1000. The funds are managed by experts who have the research facilities and up-to-the-minute information needed to take advantage of changes in the marketplace. The funds are diversified, with money invested in many different types of bonds and corporations, so that the degree of risk is minimized. And the money you invest remains liquid.

The chief disadvantage of such a fund is the management fee you must pay, which usually amounts to about 1 percent of your investment annually. However, if the fund is a well-managed one, this price is worth paying. Before you sign on, investigate the fund as fully as possible. Study the prospectus carefully. Check the current portfolio of holdings; you'll probably want to insist that all the bonds owned carry A ratings or better, although investors seeking exceptionally high returns may be willing to take a chance on lower-rated bonds. Investigate the fund's past performance, up to 10 years back if possible; a well-run fund should usually outperform the market average. And find out how frequently the fund distributed income. Monthly payments will yield you a greater return than semiannual or annual ones.

To summarize: Bonds make an excellent choice for many middle-income investors, especially those whose primary need is for income, rather than growth. Older people looking toward retirement, for example, are likely to find bonds a particularly attractive investment. However, since bonds are available in so many different forms, be careful in your selections. Remember the importance of safety, and use the standard ratings as your guide. And be sure you understand the details of the particular bond issue you are considering before you buy. The informed investor can do very well in today's corporate bond market. Happy hunting!

Gold, Silver, and Diamonds

· ·

Although they're not the best investment choice for everyone, precious gems and metals exert a unique fascination.

Gold has been used as money since biblical times. It has several characteristics which have made it desirable as a medium of exchange. Gold is scarce. It is durable: More than 95 percent of all the gold ever mined is still in circulation. And it is inherently valuable because of its beauty and its usefulness in industrial and decorative applications. Half a century ago, the right to own gold bullion was taken away from the U.S. public. That right was restored, in part, in 1975. Now, many investors regard gold as a useful hedge against inflation, and you may want to consider owning gold as part of your own investment program.

Gold has long been referred to as the "doomsday metal," because of its traditional role as a bulwark against economic, social, and political upheaval and the resulting loss of confidence in other investments, even those guaranteed by national governments. However, gold's traditional role is changing. Many now consider it a sound investment option regardless of the vagaries of the economy. On this basis, gold can be judged as an investment, just like stocks and bonds. And just as with stocks and bonds, it's necessary to understand something about how the value of gold fluctuates in order to form an effective investment plan.

The value of gold changes daily, due to economic and political conditions. When interest rates in the United States fall, the dollar grows weaker in relation to other currencies. As a result, foreign businesspeople find U.S. investments less attractive, and some of them turn to gold instead. This forces the price of gold higher. When interest rates in the United States rise, the reverse occurs: The dollar grows stronger, investments in the United States increase, and the relative value of gold falls.

As an example, consider the summer of 1981. It was a period of soaring inflation coupled with extremely high interest rates offered by the money markets and the U.S. Treasury. Consequently, money market investments and Treasury obligations became very attractive to investors, since they were both highly liquid and highly lucrative. The same period witnessed a sharp decline in the price of gold.

The value of gold, then, is quite volatile. Investing in gold carries with it a definite degree of risk. Any number of events which investors cannot control could influence the price of gold. Many government actions, such as a decision by the U.S. Treasury to sell some of its vast gold holdings, could cause a sharp drop in the price of gold. Even a soaring gold price can carry risks for the investor. If the price of gold becomes prohibitively high, industrial users of the metal may turn to substitutes. This could quickly increase the supply of gold relative to demand and so force the price down. Risks such as these must be considered before you decide to invest in gold.

There's one more drawback to investing in gold. Gold

is a non-income-producing asset. That is, it earns profits only when it is sold for a price greater than its purchase price. Gold earns no interest while it sits in your vault. Therefore, gold should be purchased as an investment only by people who have no need of investment income and who have time to watch the market and sell at an advantage. This is why gold has been compared to real estate: As an investment, it is easy to get into but difficult to leave.

Despite these drawbacks, gold is an attractive investment for many. During its strong periods, gold has been known to increase in value many times over a short span of weeks or months. And, of course, gold has a strong aesthetic and emotional appeal. Unlike most other investments, gold can serve not only as a source of security for the future but also as an ornament to be worn today.

Pure gold is known as 24-karat (24K) gold. In this form, it is too soft to be made into jewelry. Therefore, it is generally mixed with other metals, such as zinc, copper, nickel, and silver, for additional strength. The number of karats marked on an item of jewelry indicates the ratio of gold to other metals contained in the piece; the higher the karat rating, the more gold the item contains (and the higher its price is likely to be). For example, 18K gold contains 18 parts gold, 6 parts other metals; 14K gold contains 14 parts gold, 10 parts other metals. This means that 14K jewelry is only 58% gold.

There are several different methods of investing in gold. Let's consider each in turn.

Gold Bullion: When you buy gold bullion, you are buying gold in the form of bars that are 99.9% pure gold. You can actually take physical possession of the gold bars, or you can buy the gold through a bank or broker that stores the gold in its own secure facilities. Although you can buy as little as an ounce of gold bullion, a minimum of 10 ounces is usually required, with a kilo bar (32.15 ounces) being the standard.

When you buy gold bullion, you must pay certain charges apart from the ounce-for-ounce value of the gold. A charge of $15 to $30 per ounce for casting and assaying is typical. In addition, some banks may charge for holding your gold a storage fee as high as 1 percent of its value per month.

If you have gold bullion stored by a bank or broker, make certain that it is in a totally "non-fungible" storage program. This means that your gold is not combined with the assets of others but rather held separately and labeled with your name. Under such an arrangement, you have legal title to the gold, and it cannot be considered part of the assets of the bank or dealer which could be tied up by creditors in case of a liquidation.

Gold Coins: Coins are a popular form for the purchase of gold. They are not only valuable but attractive, and since they are small and portable, they can be kept in a safe in your home or in any bank vault. Most gold coins are minted to weigh 1 ounce, but some weighing as little as $\frac{1}{10}$ ounce are available. Expect to pay between 5 and 17 percent beyond the value of the gold to cover the expense of minting and retail costs. Popular foreign gold coins include the Kruggerand, produced in South Africa, the Corona (Australia), the gold peso (Mexico), and the Maple Leaf (Canada).

Gold Options: When you buy a gold option through a broker, you are buying a contract which gives you the right to buy gold at a specific price on a specific date in the future. The person selling the option promises to deliver the gold at the specified price on the specified date. Therefore, it makes sense to buy gold options at a time when you believe that the price of gold is about to increase. The standard gold option contract is for 100 ounces of gold traded on the New York Commodities Exchange.

Gold Stocks: These are shares in companies whose business is gold mining. The purchase of gold stocks is a way of betting on the future price of gold without actually dealing in the metal itself. Gold stocks have some advantages over owning gold directly. Securities are more liquid than the metal, and no assaying or storage costs are involved. However, shares in gold-mining companies are "leveraged instruments." That is, the value of the stock is affected disproportionately by the value of the product being sold. When the value of gold rises, the value of the stock rises even faster, but when the value of gold falls, the value of gold stock falls faster and farther. In addition, gold stocks pay no dividends, and when the gold originates in a foreign country, they may be subject to risks due to uncertain political, military, and economic conditions.

Gold Certificates: If you want to buy a small amount of gold (minimum around $2500) and do not want to take delivery, certain banks and brokers will allow you to make a purchase and receive a certificate of ownership, rather than the gold itself. In essence, you are buying title to gold held at a bank or broker on your behalf. A yearly fee of about ½ percent is usually charged. The main advantage of this way of buying gold is that you do not need to have the gold assayed when you decide to sell it. This makes your assets more liquid.

Silver, like gold, is a precious metal sometimes considered as an investment option. Due to its lower price, silver has been called "the poor man's gold." But don't sneer at silver. Although both gold and silver tend to benefit from periods of inflation, silver has the advantage over gold in some respects. Where gold's primary role is monetary, silver's is industrial. Silver has many more commercial uses than gold—Kodak, for example, uses huge amounts of silver every year in manufacturing photographic film—and because of its unique physical and chemical properties, no substitute for silver seems likely to be devised. These industrial uses provide a solid foundation for the future value of silver.

The ratio of the price of gold to the price of silver is a useful investment guideline for those interested in buying either of these metals. You can easily determine the current gold/silver ratio by dividing this morning's gold price by that of silver. For years, the average gold/silver ratio has been 32:1. A high or low gold/silver ratio indicates that one of the metals is currently undervalued in relation to the other, and you will want to consider moving your holdings into the undervalued metal. For example, a gold/silver ratio of 40:1 shows that silver is undervalued and therefore the metal to buy. A ratio of 15:1 means "Buy gold."

As with gold, there are several ways to buy silver. One way is to buy "junk silver," which consists of a bag of pre-1965 U.S. dimes, quarters, and half-dollars with a face value of $1000 and a market value based upon the price of silver for the day. Silver bullion is available in 1000-ounce bars. Silver certificates are receipts for the purchase of silver held at a bank in your name. Like gold certificates, silver certificates have the advantages of being highly liquid and posing no storage or security problems.

As an investment, **diamonds** have a great deal in common with gold. Both gold and diamonds tend to be costly in terms of broker's fees and sales markups, but both offer the investor safety and a hedge against inflation. Diamonds are also a good hedge against depression. Have you ever seen what happens when you give a diamond to a depressed spouse?

For people with substantial wealth who wish to concentrate a lot of that wealth in a small space, diamonds can be a sound investment. Unlike gold, diamonds don't demand continual monitoring of a highly volatile market; diamond prices don't fluctuate wildly. However, there are too many drawbacks associated with diamonds for them to be considered a viable investment option for middle-income people. Here's why:

1. Most diamonds appreciate in value less than 8 percent a year.

2. Like gold, diamonds are non-income-producing; no interest or dividends are paid on diamonds.

3. Diamonds are relatively difficult to liquidate.

4. The jewelry value of a diamond is much higher than its investment value because of heavy retail markups, which range from 40 to 300 percent, with 100 percent being the average. A diamond bought from a jeweler for $8000 is likely to yield only about $4000 if you decide to sell it to another jeweler later.

5. Storing and insuring diamonds are costly.

6.   About 85 percent of the world's diamond market is controlled by the DeBeers-Central Selling Organization, headquartered in London. Therefore, the price of diamonds is dependent on the activities of a single group, which is probably not a desirable investment situation.

If you do decide to buy diamonds for investment purposes, regard it as a long-term proposal, not a get-rich-quick scheme. Buy gems weighing from 1 to 3 carats and have them evaluated by an appraiser from the Gemological Institute of America (GIA). Once your diamond's GIA certificate is received, its fair price can easily be determined, since the certificate will state the gem's color, cut, clarity, and weight. Based on these four factors, the diamond's price can be found by using tables prepared by GIA.

The four factors mentioned above—sometimes called "the four Cs"—are the determining factors of the quality and value of a diamond. Look for them when considering the purchase of a gem. A reputable jeweler will answer your questions about a stone in terms of these four factors.

Color refers to how white or yellow a diamond is. The color of a diamond is rated alphabetically from D to Z. The closer a diamond is to the D grade, the whiter its color and the more valuable the stone. *Cut* refers to the shape of the diamond and the skill with which it has been crafted. The brilliance and beauty of a diamond depend largely on how accurately the diamond-cutter did his or her job. Note that round diamonds are generally the most valuable; other cuts are usually worth from 10 to 30 percent less by weight. *Clarity* refers to the number and size of the flaws (or "inclusions") contained in the stone. It takes an expert with a magnifying glass to rate the clarity of a stone.

Diamonds range from flawless (FL) to imperfect (L-1, L-2). The fourth C is *carat,* the common measurement of the weight of a gem. One carat weighs $1/142$ of an ounce. The value of a diamond increases dramatically as its size increases; a 2-carat stone will usually be worth more than twice as much as a 1-carat stone of comparable quality.

To summarize: Gold, silver, and diamonds probably have more drawbacks than advantages as investment options for the average middle-class American. If you want to try your hand at investing in them, go ahead; if you educate yourself and follow the market carefully, you may do very well. But most people will probably derive more benefit from the beauty and sentimental value of gold, silver, and diamond objects than they will from their investment value.

Government-Insured Mortgages (Ginnie Maes)

••

Ginnie Maes provide a secure source of income and high yields guaranteed by Uncle Sam; but the ins and outs of this relatively new financial instrument can be confusing for the novice.

As you know if you've even dipped a toe into the housing market, home mortgage rates are currently quite high. For the home buyer, this is a problem, but for the investor, it can be an opportunity. By investing in home mortgages, you can reap some of the benefits of the high interest rates being paid on mortgage loans. Ginnie Maes offer a way for the small- to medium-sized investor to get involved in this area with minimal risk. Here's what this colorfully nicknamed, little-understood investment is all about.

In 1968, Congress established the Government National Mortgage Association (GNMA) as a branch of the Department of Housing and Urban Development. The mission of GNMA is to buy government-insured mortgages, like those guaranteed by the Federal Housing Administration (FHA) and the Veterans Administration (VA), from the banks which originally made the loans. By doing this, GNMA provides the lending institutions with the money to offer additional mortgages.

After buying these FHA and VA mortgages, GNMA groups them into units of a million dollars or more, known as *pools*. These pools are then sold to investment brokerage houses, with an additional guarantee against default added by GNMA. The brokers, in turn, sell shares in these pools to the public normally in units of $25,000 or more. These shares are known as ***Ginnie Mae pass-through certificates***. The name "Ginnie Mae" is a fanciful pronunciation of GNMA, and the term "pass-through certificate" comes from the fact that, when an investor buys the certificate, the homeowner's mortgage payments are passed through to the investor.

As you see, then, the Ginnie Mae is a way of investing in a large pool of government-guaranteed mortgages simply by purchasing a share in the pool. Since the smallest units sold are $25,000 packages, institutional investors do most of the direct trading in Ginnie Maes. However, as you'll read about later, it's possible to get involved in Ginnie Maes for as little as $1000 by buying a unit in a Ginnie Mae mutual fund or trust.

Ginnie Maes are an extremely safe investment. Because of the involvement of GNMA, payments of both principal and interest on the mortgage loans are fully guaranteed by the federal government. This guarantee is on top of the government guarantee which already covers FHA and VA mortgages. So the degree of risk in Ginnie Maes is as small as you're ever likely to get.

Income from Ginnie Maes is paid on a monthly basis. If you own a Ginnie Mae, you'll receive a check around the fifteenth of each month representing an installment of the repayment of the mortgages in the pool you've bought into. A part of each check represents repayment of the principal on the loan; the rest is interest. An enclosed statement will tell you what portion of the check is interest and what portion is principal—something you'll need to know, since the interest portion is taxable by the federal, state, and local governments, while the principal payments are not. During the early months of the repayment period, you'll mainly receive interest; later payments include a higher percentage of principal.

There is a variation on this system by which you can arrange to have the principal remain intact and receive only interest payments. Younger investors may wish to consider this option. It provides for steady payments of interest on a fixed principal, which itself is paid in full at the time when the certificate matures. Older investors— retirees, for example—will probably prefer the usual interest-plus-principal repayment plan, since they usually have a greater need for monthly income than for a large lump-sum payment at the end.

There is one major drawback to investing in Ginnie Maes. The monthly checks you'll receive will vary in size, and the period over which the checks keep coming may vary too. The reason is that no one knows for sure when the mortgages will be paid off. As you know, some people take a full 30 years to repay their mortgage loans; others sell their houses and repay the mortgages after only a year or two. Since no one can predict how long the homeowners in a particular pool will take to repay their loans, no one can predict exactly how long the payments will last or how large each monthly payment will be.

One rule of thumb brokers often cite is that Ginnie Mae mortgage pools are repaid, on the average, within 12 years. This means that if you buy a Ginnie Mae certificate, you can estimate that you'll continue to receive monthly checks for about 12 years; and those checks will be larger in the beginning than near the end, since the amount of outstanding debt will be greater at that time. Neither prediction is guaranteed. For example, your certificate may continue to pay monthly checks for 15 years or more; on the other hand, it may be entirely paid out within 5 to 8 years, or even less.

Changes in the market interest rate on mortgages play an important role here. The interest rate you'll receive on your Ginnie Mae depends, of course, on the mortgage rate at the time the pool was established. If mortgage rates fall below that figure, it's likely that repayment of your Ginnie Mae will be accelerated. This is because the homeowners who took out the mortgages will be eager to repay their high-interest loans and refinance their homes at the new, lower rates. So you'll get back your money sooner and be forced to reinvest it elsewhere at the new, lower prevailing interest rates.

By contrast, if mortgage rates rise, the life of your Ginnie Mae is likely to be prolonged. Homeowners will be content to keep paying the relatively low rate of interest they locked in at the time they took out their mortgages, and you'll continue to receive checks for longer than the average 12-year repayment period.

As you can see, Ginnie Maes are not an ideal investment for those who *must* be able to predict their future monthly income with absolute certainty. If you can afford to be flexible, you can afford to consider Ginnie Maes.

There is a major secondary market in Ginnie Maes made up of shares in mortgage pools established at some time in the past. Like previously issued bonds, previously issued Ginnie Maes fluctuate in value due to market conditions. Depending on the age of the certificate, the number of monthly payments that have already been made, and interest rate considerations, you may be able to buy an older Ginnie Mae certificate at a considerable discount off its face value. Ginnie Mae prices are quoted as a percentage of face value. A Ginnie Mae quoted at 90 sells for 90 percent of its face value; that is, a $25,000 certificate would cost $22,500. Ginnie Mae prices tend to fluctuate less than those of bonds because of the monthly payments received.

In addition to the quoted price, there are two important factors to consider when you look at previously issued Ginnie Maes: the *pool factor* and the *pool speed.*

The pool factor is the percentage of the principal that remains unpaid in a particular mortgage pool. The higher the pool factor, the longer it will probably take for the loan repayments to be completed and the longer your checks will keep on coming. The pool speed is the relative speed with which repayment of the loans in a particular pool is occurring. This will vary depending on economic conditions, the interest rate at the time the pool was established, and the geographic areas in which the mortgages were issued. If the pool speed is high, your Ginnie Mae checks will probably end fairly soon; if the pool speed is low, they will probably last longer. The broker handling a particular certificate should be able to tell you the pool factor and pool speed on that issue.

Ginnie Maes offer a high degree of safety, along with attractive yields and good liquidity—you can sell a Ginnie Mae through your broker at any time. However, many people can't afford the $25,000 minimum investment required to buy a Ginnie Mae certificate. If you're one of these people, consider buying a unit in a Ginnie Mae mutual fund or trust. These units usually sell for $1000, and can be bought and sold through brokers. Each fund has its own rules and procedures, which you should investigate before buying, as well as its own portfolio of mortgage holdings, which may affect the income you'll receive.

When you invest in a Ginnie Mae fund, you may have to pay a sales charge of up to 3.5 percent. There may be instead, or in addition, an annual service or management fee. As with any mutual fund, shop around and ask questions before writing a check.

When you investigate Ginnie Maes, you may hear references to two other forms of mortgage-backed securities: *Freddie Macs* and *Fannie Maes.* We'll say just a word or two about these newer and less popular investments.

Freddie Macs are issued by the Federal Home Loan Mortgage Corporation (FHLMC). You can invest a minimum of $25,000 in Freddie Mac *participation certificates* (PCs). The mortgages in the Freddie Mac pools are usually not government-insured loans, like the FHA and VA mortgages in which Ginnie Mae specializes. Instead, they are privately issued and nonguaranteed mortgages. As a consequence, FHLMC does not absolutely guarantee your investment, as Ginnie Mae does; instead, you are guaranteed "timely" payments of interest and "ultimate" repayment of principal. It's possible, then, that you might be kept waiting for some of your money when you invest in a Freddie Mac. As with most forms of investment, the slightly greater risk with a Freddie Mac is counterbalanced by a higher rate of return. So Freddie Macs are by no means a dangerous or speculative investment. Note, however, that the market for Freddie Macs is much smaller than that for Ginnie Maes, so it might take a while to liquidate your holdings if and when you decide to sell.

Finally, Fannie Maes are issued by the Federal National Mortgage Association. In most ways, Fannie Maes are similar to Freddie Macs. As with Ginnie Maes, timely payments of both interest and principal are guaranteed.

However, the full credit of the federal government does *not* stand behind this guarantee, making it somewhat less unshakeable. Ginnie Maes remain the most popular—and, for most people, the most attractive—method of investing in mortgage-backed securities.

The Individual Retirement Account

●●●

Not a single type of investment but a way of saving for your retirement while you reduce your current taxes, the IRA is one savings plan that few middle-income investors can afford to be without.

The **individual retirement account** (**IRA**) is a method of investing originally designed to help individuals not covered by company pension plans save for their retirement. On January 1, 1982, the law governing IRAs was changed to make them available to anyone with earned income, whether or not the individual is covered by a company pension plan. (*Earned income* includes wages, fees, and earnings from self-employment or part-time work; it doesn't include nonemployment sources of income, such as interest or dividends.) So the chances are very good that you are currently eligible to open an IRA. As you're about to learn, the benefits of having an IRA are so impressive that it's an opportunity you won't want to pass up.

First, some basic ground rules. Your IRA is a savings account containing funds that can be invested in any of a number of different financial instruments. (We'll offer some advice on your options in a moment.) By law, you may contribute to your IRA up to 100 percent of the first $2000 that you earn each year. If a husband and wife are both working, they can each establish an IRA and contribute up to $2000 per year to each account, for a family total of $4000. If one spouse does not work, up to $2250 may be contributed, with a maximum of $2000 in one account.

The money you contribute is deducted from your income for tax purposes, providing immediate tax benefits. Furthermore, the interest or dividends your IRA earns are also tax-free. Therefore, if you contribute to your IRA every year, you'll find your account growing surprisingly quickly, as the tax-free contributions and tax-free compound earnings mount up.

Note, too, that there's some flexibility as to when you make your tax-free contribution. You can open or add money to an IRA at any time during the calendar year or up to April 15 of the following year and still qualify for the annual tax deduction. For example, you can save on your 1986 taxes by contributing to an IRA any time from January 1, 1986, through April 15, 1987.

Since the IRA was created specifically to make it easier for working people to save for retirement, there are built-in restrictions on your access to IRA funds. You can begin withdrawing your IRA money without penalty after reaching age 59½. If you must withdraw the money before that time, you will have to pay an extra 10 percent tax on the amount you withdraw as a penalty, unless you're disabled.

The penalty for early withdrawal deters many young people from opening IRAs. When you're 25 years old, age 59½ may seem an eternity away, and over 30 years may seem like an impossibly long time to tie up your money. However, the effects of the penalty aren't nearly as severe as you might think. Because of the tax benefits derived both at the time of the contribution and during the accumulation of tax-free interest, IRA accounts become profitable fairly quickly even when taking into account the penalty for early withdrawal. With 5 or 6 years of compounding, your income will more than compensate for the withdrawal penalty. After that time, even if you incur the 10 percent penalty, you will have increased your money faster than otherwise possible because of the tax benefits. Therefore, don't let the early withdrawal penalty discourage you unduly. An IRA is still a highly beneficial investment to have.

You *must* begin withdrawing your IRA funds by the time you reach age 70½. As you withdraw the funds, they are taxable as regular income for that year. However, your income will probably be lower after you retire, and the rate at which you'll be taxed will be lower as well.

You can withdraw the money in a lump sum or in installments, as you wish. If you choose the installment method, you must follow a schedule based on your life expectancy as determined by standard actuarial tables. For example, a 70-year-old man has a life expectancy of 12 years; a 70-year-old woman, 15 years. Therefore, the 70-year-old man who wishes to begin withdrawing his IRA funds must withdraw ¹⁄₁₂ of his total account each year, while the woman must withdraw ¹⁄₁₅ of her account. The penalty for failing to follow this schedule is stiff: For every dollar you fail to withdraw on schedule, you lose 50 cents.

There are two notable variations on this withdrawal scheme. In 1985, the law was modified to allow you to refigure your life expectancy each year. Since the older you get, the greater your expected age of demise becomes, annually refiguring your life expectancy will allow you to reduce the fraction that must be withdrawn from your IRA each year.

A second change in the law allows you to extend your IRA withdrawal period to cover the combined life expect-

ancy of you and your spouse. This figure will usually be
higher than the life expectancy of either husband or wife.
For example, a 70-year-old man is expected to live 12
years, and a 70-year-old woman 15 years. However, one or
the other can be expected to survive for 18 years. Therefore, the 70-year-old couple can use the 18-year life expectancy figure as the basis of their withdrawals if they
wish—and they can recalculate their combined life expectancy each year as well.

Most retirees choose to withdraw their IRA funds on
the installment basis. However, you may want to consider
withdrawing the money, when available, as a lump sum
and using that cash to purchase an annuity which will
provide guaranteed annual payments for the rest of your
life. (See the section "Annuities" for more information.)

What happens if you die before you get a chance to use
your IRA funds? There are several possibilities. When you
start an IRA, you designate a beneficiary. If you die, your
beneficiary may choose any of the following options:

1. Your beneficiary can withdraw the IRA funds as a
    lump sum. The entire amount would be taxable
    during that year.

2. Your beneficiary can withdraw the IRA funds over
    a period of 5 years. During each of those years, the
    amount withdrawn that year is taxable.

3. Your beneficiary can withdraw the IRA funds and
    use them to purchase an annuity. The money
    would only be taxable at the time annuity benefits
    are paid.

4. Your beneficiary can convert the IRA into his or
    her own account. The new owner will have all the
    rights and obligations you had. Some IRA agree-

ments do not allow this option, so ask your bank or broker before you open your account.

You now understand the basic rules that govern IRAs: how contributions are made, how withdrawals occur, and what tax benefits you can expect. Now let's consider the various investment options you have to choose from when opening your IRA.

When you invest in an IRA, the law requires that a trustee be named to administer the account. The trustee must file reports with you and with the federal government. Typical IRA trustees include commercial and savings banks, savings and loan institutions, brokerage houses, insurance companies, and other types of investment firms.

As for the type of investment, any of a wide range of choices may be suitable for your IRA, depending on your age and financial status and the degree of risk you wish to take. The only restrictions on IRA investments are these: You may not invest your IRA funds in collectibles, such as postage stamps, coins, precious metals, antiques, or art; you may not invest your IRA in life insurance contracts; and you may not make an investment in which you have a direct interest, as, for example, if you were to buy a home with IRA funds and then rent it from the IRA account. Here are some of the most popular investment choices for IRA accounts:

Banks and Savings and Loan Institutions: An IRA bank account usually takes the form of a certificate of deposit with a minimum term of 18 months. Rates may be either fixed in advance or variable. If rates are variable, find out how the rate is set and how often it is adjusted—weekly, monthly, or whatever.

In general, the most conservative investment strategy is to invest for the shortest available term. You may lose slightly if interest rates decline, but you stand to gain if they rise; on the whole, the flexibility of being able to move your funds fairly frequently is an important asset.

As you add to your IRA year by year, you may find your account approaching the $100,000 amount, which is the maximum covered by federal deposit insurance. Don't worry. You can make sure that you're covered even when you exceed the maximum by taking the excess amount and opening a second IRA at a different bank. The $100,000 maximum includes only the funds you deposit at a single financial institution.

Stocks and Bonds: If you wish, you can deposit your IRA money with a stockbroker, who will act as your trustee. However, you direct the account yourself: You make your own investment decisions and you can buy and sell stocks and bonds, moving your funds from one investment to another, without incurring any taxes on the money.

If you know the stock or bond markets and are willing to accept a degree of risk, investing your IRA in this fashion may be a reasonable choice. But the same strictures that normally apply to investing in stocks and bonds apply with added force to using your IRA for this purpose. Analyze your personal risk tolerance before taking this route. If you are young, this option may be attractive to you; the longer you have until retirement, the more time you'll have to make up for any investment mistakes you make. On the other hand, if you are already nearing retirement age, a more conservative form of investment would probably be better.

Mutual Funds: You can deposit your IRA money in a mutual fund, and so invest not in a few self-selected stocks but in a managed portfolio of many issues put together by a brokerage firm. Mutual funds vary widely; some specialize in government-backed securities, others in the blue-chip stocks, and still others in riskier—but potentially more lucrative—issues. You may wish to choose a broker that offers a "family of funds" of different types among which you are free to switch your investment from time to time without charge or penalty.

If you want to invest your IRA in a mutual fund, bear in mind that your investment will not be insured and will be subject to many of the same risks incurred in any stock market investment program. You will have to pay a service fee to the company that manages the fund and, in some cases, a sales charge known as a "load" is imposed. Since loads can be hefty, look for one of the so-called no-load funds which impose no sales charges. Finally, remember that there's no need to invest in any of the special tax-exempt mutual funds; your IRA investment is already sheltered from all levels of taxation. Stick to the funds which are normally taxable; these usually offer a higher rate of return.

How should you choose among these investment options? One prime consideration should be how well you have otherwise provided for your retirement. If your IRA is your sole retirement plan, you should invest conservatively; if you have substantial savings outside of the IRA, income which you expect to continue after retirement, or a secure company pension plan, you can afford a bit more risk. Your age is another important factor. Here are some guidelines to use depending on your present age:

Age 20 to 40: When you are young, growth should be your primary goal; a relatively high degree of risk is tolerable. Suggestion: Invest your IRA in a diversified portfolio of common stocks or in a mutual fund managed for growth of assets, not income.

Age 40 to 50: Stocks are still an attractive choice. However, if you expect to begin withdrawing your IRA funds when you reach age 59½, redirect some of your funds away from growth stocks and into current income-generating investments.

Age 50 to 60: At this point, growth is less important, risk less acceptable. Move your investments out of stocks and into bonds, in order to minimize risk and increase your current flow of income.

Age 60 and Over: By now, all your IRA funds should be in income-producing investments with maturities of 5 years and less. This will provide safety and maximum current interest.

No matter where you decide to invest your IRA funds, you are entitled to receive certain types of information from the institution at which you opened the account. These include a copy of your contract of purchase for the IRA; a disclosure statement stating the rules and regulations applying to the account; and a chart listing the projected values of your investment if you withdraw it during any of the first 5 years of investment and at ages 60, 65, and 70. Study this material carefully before you invest. If you change your mind within 7 days after making the investment, you are entitled to withdraw your money without penalty.

Once your IRA is in operation, you can move your money from one account to another in either of two ways: *direct transfer* or *rollover*. With direct transfer, the institution holding your IRA transfers it, at your request, directly to the new account, either at the same institution or elsewhere. You may move your IRA funds by direct transfer as many times as you like to take advantage of a changing investment situation without incurring any tax penalty. The rollover method can only be used once a year. It involves your taking possession of the IRA funds for up to 60 days. By the end of that time, you must have reinvested the funds in another IRA; otherwise, you will have to pay taxes on the amount held, along with any applicable penalties.

Finally, a few more miscellaneous facts and suggestions related to IRAs:

- Try to make your IRA investment at the beginning of the year, rather than the end. You'll save on taxes this way, since the dividends or interest earned by your money in an IRA is tax-free. For example, $2000 invested in an account paying 9 percent interest will earn $180 in the course of a year. If you're in the 40 percent tax bracket, Uncle Sam will take $72 of that interest. If you deposit the money in your IRA as soon as you can, however, you'll keep all $180 for yourself.

- If you get divorced, you and your spouse will keep control of your individual IRAs. A divorced spouse who is not working and is receiving alimony can contribute to an IRA up to $2000. However, to be eligible for this, the IRA must have been started at least 5 years before the divorce and funds must have been contributed to the account in at least 3 of those 5 years.

- It's often a good idea to borrow money to use in opening an IRA. For example, suppose you take out a 1-year loan of $2000 and deposit that money in an IRA. First, your taxable income for the year will be reduced by the $2000 IRA investment, thus saving you money on taxes. Second, the interest you pay on the loan is tax-deductible, shaving your tax bill still more. Your monthly loan repayments become a form of forced savings—the only kind of savings some people can manage. Saving the money for your IRA in advance is still cheaper than borrowing it, but borrowing the money for an IRA is better than not opening an IRA at all.

The Keogh Plan

If you're self-employed, you can save on your taxes today while saving for retirement tomorrow by establishing a Keogh plan account.

The **Keogh plan,** also called the **HR-10 plan,** is a form of pension plan designed for the self-employed individual. It is named after Representative Eugene Keogh, who sponsored the original legislation that created the Keogh plan in 1963.

A Keogh plan account is similar to an individual retirement account (IRA) in several ways. Your annual contribution to a Keogh account reduces your taxable income, and the sums in your account grow tax-free until you withdraw them upon retirement. As with an IRA, you may withdraw your investment after reaching the age of 59½; the upper limit on withdrawal is age 70½. At that time, the sums you withdraw are treated as ordinary taxable income. However, your income will probably be substantially lower after retirement, so that the size of your tax bite will be much smaller. Early withdrawals prior to age 59½ carry a 10 percent penalty. Therefore, as with an IRA, you should invest in a Keogh account only sums you don't expect to need until retirement. Liquidity is not one of the characteristics of a Keogh account.

However, there are significant differences between a Keogh account and an IRA. As we'll explain in a moment, not everyone is eligible for a Keogh account. While the maximum amount you may contribute to an IRA in any year is $2000, you may invest up to a maximum of $30,000 or 25 percent of your earned income, whichever is less, in a Keogh account.

Withdrawals from the two types of accounts are also handled differently. With both an IRA and a Keogh account, you can withdraw the money either in a lump sum upon retirement or in installments. However, if you withdraw your Keogh investment in a lump sum, you can take advantage of the *10-year forward averaging rule,* which allows you to compute your taxable income as if the withdrawal had been spread out over a 10-year period. With an IRA, the averaging period is restricted to 5 years. Thus the Keogh plan can produce significantly greater income tax savings at withdrawal time than the IRA.

In order to qualify for a Keogh account, you must be self-employed as either the sole proprietor of a business, an unincorporated professional, or a partner in an unincorporated partnership. In addition, if your business has any employees, you are required to include in the plan all those who have worked for you longer than 3 years. You must contribute to their retirement funds the same percentage of their salary that you are contributing to your own. (Naturally, the employer's share of the Keogh investment is treated as a deductible business expense.) The Keogh account may be invested in almost any kind of investment favored by the employer, including a bank deposit, stocks and bonds, a money market fund, or an insurance account. Collectibles are virtually the only common type of investment not allowed. The employer may choose to manage the Keogh personally or may invest the money in an annuity contract purchased from an insurance company or a mutual fund managed by a broker.

Ever since their introduction, Keoghs have been among the most popular pension plans. In 1984, the contribution limits were raised from $15,000 or 15 percent of earned income to the present $30,000 or 25 percent. This change has only increased the attractiveness of the Keogh plan. If you're eligible for a Keogh plan account, you should certainly give it serious consideration as an investment option. It is a kind of super IRA which allows the self-employed professional or business proprietor to reduce his or her current taxable income while saving a substantial sum toward retirement.

Life Insurance

••

There is a wide variety of insurance plans available, some of which offer surprising benefits for investors.

The basic purpose of *life insurance* is to offer financial protection to your loved ones in the event of your death. The benefit it provides is one you hope you won't need—at least, not soon—but which most people would be foolish to do without. This is what life insurance is for, and the needs of your beneficiaries in case you die should be your main consideration in purchasing life insurance for yourself.

However, many life insurance policies also contain investment features which can be used to provide additional income for you and your family. You probably won't want to buy life insurance primarily for its investment value—other forms of investment are generally more lucrative—but the investment benefits can be a significant secondary reason for buying insurance, as well as a factor in choosing among the available policies. So it pays to understand the different types of life insurance and their varying values as investments.

Let's consider the five most popular forms of life insurance today, with special attention to their investment potential: term insurance, straight life insurance, limited-payment life insurance, endowment insurance, and universal life insurance.

Term Insurance: Term life insurance offers the greatest amount of financial protection at the lowest cost in premiums. This is because when you buy term insurance, you buy the possible death benefit only; there is no savings or investment feature. The policy simply guarantees payment of a specified sum if you die during the life of the policy (the "term" from which this type of insurance gets its name). Term policies are usually issued for a specific period of years, after which the insurance coverage can be renewed but only at a higher premium rate.

Two variations on the term insurance policy are the *decreasing term* policy, in which the premiums remain the same but the amount of the death benefit decreases as you get older, and the *level term* policy, in which the amount of the death benefit remains the same but the size of the premium increases over time.

Term insurance is popular in instances where the need for life insurance protection is temporary or where other, more costly forms of insurance are unaffordable. For example, term insurance may be an ideal choice for a young family with children, where insurance protection is vital but the family income may still be modest. As the family grows older and the parents' careers take wing, the family income will probably increase, and other types of policies may become more attractive.

Straight Life Insurance: Also known as "whole life insurance," a straight life policy offers a specified death benefit (the face value of the policy) in exchange for an unchanging premium payment. The size of the premium depends mainly on your age at the time you purchase the policy; the younger you are, the lower your annual premium will be. At the time of your death, the face value of the policy will be paid to your beneficiary.

Unlike term insurance, straight life insurance includes an investment feature. Part of your premium payment is placed in a savings fund and invested by the insurance company. As the years pass, the amount of money in this fund will grow both from your contributions and from the company's investment earnings. This growing sum is known as the policy's *cash surrender value.* It is quite small at first but, after a number of years, can become a substantial amount of money. The cash surrender value of your policy can benefit you in two ways. First, if you terminate the policy, you can receive the cash surrender value as a lump sum (unlike term insurance, where you walk away with nothing). Second, while the policy is in force, you can borrow against the cash surrender value at a favorable interest rate, even if you may not qualify for other types of loans. This provision can be useful, for example, when college tuition bills come due.

The investment value of straight life insurance gives it an advantage over term insurance. However, it is considerably more costly. The amount of savings you'll accumulate through your insurance policy is probably smaller than the amount you could save through other investment plans. And, of course, in order for your beneficiary to receive the death benefit, you must continue to pay premiums until you die. This can be a financial strain, especially for older people whose earnings have fallen after retirement. So consider the pros and cons carefully before opting for a straight life policy.

Limited-Payment Life Insurance: As with straight life, a limited-payment policy provides for payment of a specified death benefit whenever you die. However, premium payments are made for only a limited number of years, usually 20. Naturally, the premiums are higher, although the cash surrender value of a limited-payment life policy is generally greater than that of a straight life policy. If you anticipate a continuing need for insurance protection combined with a foreseeable drop in your income, you may want to consider the limited-payment life policy as an insurance option.

Endowment Insurance: An endowment policy provides both insurance protection and substantial investment value. Premiums are paid for a specified number of years, during which, if you die, the face value of the policy will be paid to your beneficiary. If you survive to the end of the endowment period, you receive as a lump sum the full face value of the policy. An endowment policy may be worth considering if you want to combine protection with saving for a specific, foreseeable future need, such as educational expenses or retirement. However, the endowment policy has its drawbacks. The premiums are high. For the same money, far more insurance protection could be purchased through either term or straight life. And greater savings growth and more flexibility can usually be obtained through a universal life policy, as described below.

Universal Life Insurance: First introduced in 1979, universal life is a new type of life insurance which combines insurance protection (in the form of term insurance coverage) with a savings plan that builds tax-deferred income at highly competitive rates. The holder of a universal life policy chooses the amount of life insurance protection he or she wants, and part of the premium goes to cover that protection. The rest of the premium payment is invested by the insurance company in various high-yielding investments. The policy is very flexible. At any time the amount of insurance coverage can be increased or decreased, the size of the premiums can be adjusted, and the accumulated cash value can be withdrawn by means of an automatic policy loan.

Of course, when you buy a universal life policy, you cannot decide where your investment dollars will go; that decision rests in the hands of the insurance company's investment managers. If the managers make a series of bad investment decisions, the cash value of your policy will decline. This can't happen with straight life insurance, where cash values are projected using a fixed interest rate, so that you know in advance just what your policy's cash surrender value will be at any time.

Therefore, when shopping for universal life insurance, it's very important to compare the investment policies of different insurance companies. Some are more successful than others. Also find out about the fees charged by the companies you're considering. Some charge heavy sales commissions, which may run as high as 50 percent of your first year's premium; others charge large surrender fees (known as "back-end loads") in the event you decide to cancel your policy. Ask before you buy. And study the company's annual report, which should list all expenses incurred, premiums paid, and interest credited on universal life accounts.

One more point: Stay away from universal life unless you have at least $3000 to tie up in your investment and want at least $50,000 worth of insurance coverage. If you aren't in this bracket, you'll find that universal life will cost more than it's worth, despite its relatively high investment yield.

Money Market Funds

Especially in times of high inflation, a money market fund can be a highly lucrative "parking place" for your money.

The money market is the market for buying and selling high-yield, short-term instruments of credit. In the money market, securities such as Treasury bills, bank certificates of deposit, and short-term commercial loans are bought and sold. Since these securities carry high interest rates, they make money grow quickly. But they normally require extremely large investments. That's where the **money market funds** come in. First made available in 1974, money market funds offer the small investor a chance to take advantage of the high interest rates prevailing in the money markets. Here's how it works.

Money market funds operate on the concept of pooling. By combining many small investments, the fund can accumulate the kind of money needed to buy the costly money market instruments described above. Since the instruments purchased by the fund have different maturities, the fund earns interest on a daily basis. Each investor receives his or her share of the interest by means of a regular statement, usually issued monthly. The amount earned on an investment varies continually as the prevalent interest rates in the money market rise and fall.

Money market funds are managed by investment firms and brokerage houses. Most transact business by mail, so a money market fund headquartered in Boston, for example, may have shareholders in any of the 50 states. A minimum deposit is required to open a money market account; $1000 is a typical minimum amount. You can add to your investment at any time, and your funds are completely liquid—you can make withdrawals whenever you wish. Many money market funds allow you to withdraw your money simply by writing a check. Thus you may want to consider using a money market fund in place of a conventional checking account.

Money market funds can be broken down into three categories, based upon the type of instruments in which the funds are invested:

1. **General Money Market Funds:** These invest primarily in nongovernmental securities, such as bank certificates of deposit, commercial loans, bankers' acceptances, and so on. General money market funds usually pay the highest interest rates of the three categories of funds.

2. **Government-Only Money Market Funds:** These invest only in securities issued by the U.S. government or by a federal agency. These funds boast a somewhat higher degree of safety than the general money market funds, but they pay a little less.

3. **Tax-Free Money Market Funds:** These purchase only short-term, tax-exempt municipal bonds. Income from these funds is not subject to federal tax, but may be subject to state and local taxes. Tax-

free money market funds are especially suitable for investors in a high tax bracket.

Because of the liquidity of your investment in a money market fund, it makes an ideal way to invest idle cash which might otherwise find its way into a low-paying passbook savings account. For example, placing the proceeds from the sale of securities into a money market fund until you've decided upon your next investment venture is a good way of earning continuous high interest on your money.

Banks have now entered the money market field with their version of the money market fund, the *money market deposit account* (*MMDA*). The MMDA is similar in many ways to the money market fund. It, too, is based on the pooling concept, allowing small investors to earn interest rates otherwise reserved for large institutional investors or wealthy individuals. Like a money market fund, an MMDA requires a minimum initial deposit as well as a minimum balance. (If your investment falls below the minimum, the bank will pay only the passbook account rate on your money.) However, as of 1986, federal regulations will no longer require a minimum MMDA balance; banks will be free to enforce a minimum balance rule at their own discretion. Finally, like a money market fund, an MMDA is a good way to invest cash for a short period.

However, there are some significant differences between the money market fund and the MMDA. Let's consider these differences and their implications for the typical investor.

When you invest in a money market fund, you become a shareholder in the fund. You and the other shareholders receive all the income earned by the fund's investments, less a small management fee (usually about ½ percent annually). When you invest in an MMDA, on the other hand, you are not a shareholder but simply a depositor. Investors in MMDAs do not necessarily receive all the interest generated by the investments; instead, they receive whatever interest rate the bank chooses to pay. Furthermore, the bank is free to invest your money in any way it sees fit. It may even make investments that have little or nothing to do with the money market. Therefore, you have no guarantee that the interest you receive will truly reflect the money market rate.

Note, too, the difference in the way the money funds and the MMDAs usually advertise the interest rates they pay. Money market funds normally advertise the current simple interest rate being earned by the fund. (This yield can change daily as conditions in the money market change, of course; it is not guaranteed.) By contrast, banks often promote MMDAs by advertising the effective yield rate, which is usually a fraction of a point higher than the simple interest rate, due to compounding. However, the effective yield rate can be misleading. It assumes that the bank will be paying compound interest on an unchanging interest rate for a full year. This is highly unlikely to occur. So take the high effective yields claimed by banks with a grain of salt.

As with any form of investment, safety is a factor to consider. Your investment in an MMDA offered by a bank or a savings and loan institution is insured by the federal government up to $100,000. Therefore, an MMDA is about as safe as any investment can be. If safety is of overriding importance to you, choose an MMDA over a money market fund. However, you should realize that the money market funds have an excellent track record as far as safety is concerned. This is because they invest only in short-term instruments issued by such secure institutions as government agencies, large corporations, and major banks. An investor's rule of thumb is that the shorter the maturity of an investment, the lower the risk. The average maturity for the investments held by general money market funds is about 35 days; for the tax-free funds, about 65 days. Investments of this type are normally quite secure. Furthermore, the Securities and Exchange Commission (SEC) regulates the money market funds very strictly. The SEC audits each fund at least once a year, and the results are distributed to all those who have invested in the fund. So a money market fund is far from a high-risk investment.

There are one or two other differences between money market funds and MMDAs to consider. With an MMDA at a local bank, you have a person-to-person relationship with an officer whom you know, rather than the kind of anonymous, by-mail relationship usually offered by the money market funds. For some, dealing with a personal banker is psychologically important. The money market fund may be preferable if you plan on making frequent withdrawals from your account. You are usually permitted unlimited withdrawals by check from the fund. With an MMDA, there is normally a limit of three checks per month. Finally, with an MMDA, you may lose up to a month's interest if you close out your account during that period. With a money market fund, this cannot happen.

William Donoghue is probably the leading expert on money market investing today. He has summed up the advantages of the money market fund and MMDA with the letters "SLY":

Security: The principal you invest is always safe.

Liquidity: You can withdraw your money at any time without penalty.

Yield: You'll earn high interest rates that reflect up-to-date market conditions.

That combination of benefits makes money market investing one of today's most popular investment options.

Mortgages

●●●

Borrowing to finance your home has changed dramatically in recent years. Not all the changes are to your advantage!

If you're like most Americans, you either own your own home or hope to own one someday. For most people, homeownership provides greater comfort and convenience in everyday living as well as a sense of security. It also offers some very real financial benefits. Real estate represents a solid investment which has proved to be a strong hedge against inflation. And as you probably know, owning a home usually carries with it substantial tax benefits.

For most people, buying a home entails taking out a **mortgage** to help meet the cost of purchase. You are normally required to pay a percentage of the purchase price in cash; this is called the **down payment.** The remainder of the purchase price is covered by the mortgage. Your title to the house is used as security for the unpaid balance on your mortgage. This means that if you are unable to repay your mortgage, the lender has the right to **foreclose,** that is, to take possession of the property. Most mortgage loans are made by banks and savings and loan associations, though other institutions and individuals may sometimes offer mortgages.

Until fairly recently, most mortgages provided for repayment over a 10- to 30-year period in equal monthly amounts based on a fixed rate of interest. Each payment included both repayment of principal and payment of interest, with early payments representing mainly interest and later payments representing mainly principal. This was known as the *fixed* level-payment mortgage. However, the volatile economic climate of the late 1970s, and in particular the soaring interest rates, led to increased use of other types of mortgages. Two types in particular—*adjustable-rate* mortgages and *balloon* mortgages—have become especially common. The terms they offer are not usually favorable to borrowers, so you'll want to be sure that you understand them fully before you agree to accept them. Let's consider each of these newly common mortgage options in some detail.

The adjustable-rate mortgage is usually a long-term loan, providing for repayment in 25 or 30 years. It differs from the traditional fixed mortgage in that the interest rate on the loan changes at stated intervals. Thus as prevailing interest rates rise, the amount you must pay the bank each month rises too; as interest rates fall, so do your monthly payments.

The amount you must pay each month on an adjustable-rate mortgage loan depends on three factors:

1. **Interval:** The period of time between adjustments of the interest rate. Typical intervals are 6 months and 1 year.

2. **Index:** A guideline used in determining the current interest rate on the mortgage. The index will be clearly defined at the time the mortgage is

made. Any of a number of widely accepted financial guidelines may be used as an index; one typical index is the current interest rate on 6-month U.S. Treasury bills. As the index goes up or down, so does the interest rate on your mortgage, and along with it your monthly payment.

3. **Cap:** A predetermined figure limiting the movement (up or down) of the interest rate on your mortgage in any single interval. If an adjustable-rate mortgage includes a cap, the interest rate may not change by an amount greater than the cap, even though the variation in the index would normally call for a greater change. Not all adjustable-rate mortgages include a provision for a cap.

As you can see, an adjustable-rate mortgage has one major disadvantage for the borrower: It's impossible to know beforehand how large your monthly payments will be in the future. Thus much of the security of the traditional fixed-rate mortgage is forfeited with an adjustable-rate mortgage. In many cases, an adjustable-rate mortgage is offered at a lower initial interest rate than a comparable fixed-rate mortgage. However, you can't know how long this advantage will last. Therefore, most home buyers prefer the fixed-rate mortgage—if one is available.

A balloon mortgage is a short-term loan usually lasting only 2 to 5 years. At the end of that period, the entire balance of the loan is due, forcing you to refinance the loan at the current market interest rate. Thus you are at the mercy of the lender every 2 to 5 years; you must either agree to the terms the bank sets or find a new lender. Avoid the balloon mortgage if you can. It erodes the investment value of your home as a hedge against inflation, and it makes your house more difficult to sell.

As you can see, the traditional fixed level-payment mortgage is normally the most desirable kind. However, it may be difficult to obtain in some areas. Do a lot of inquiring and searching before you settle on a mortgage.

No matter which type of mortgage you obtain, you'll receive significant tax benefits during the repayment period. These benefits arise from the fact that interest payments are usually deductible from income for federal income tax purposes. This means that the portion of your monthly mortgage payment which consists of interest payment can be deducted from your taxable income. For most homeowners, that's a substantial amount—especially during the early years of the repayment period, when nearly all your monthly payment goes for interest. (Later, repayment of principal becomes an increasingly large share of the monthly bill; but your family's financial status is likely to improve over time, too, so that the gradual diminution of the tax benefit probably won't be too painful.)

If you're currently shopping for a home (and a mortgage), you should be aware of two other factors which will affect the cost of home buying: *points* and *closing costs.*

Points are one-time lump-sum charges levied by the bank at the time you buy your home. A point is 1 percent of the total amount of the loan; the bank may charge from 2 to 4 points. For example, if you take out a $60,000 mortgage from a bank which charges 4 points for the loan, you will have to pay the bank a $2400 fee at the time of purchase.

If the payment of points is properly executed, it is usually deductible from your income (as an interest payment) in the year you take out the mortgage. How can you make certain whether you will get the tax deduction? The best method is to ask the lender whether the points are considered a prepayment of interest or a service fee. Prepayment of interest is deductible, a service fee is not.

If the bank certifies that the points represent a prepayment of interest, make doubly sure of your deduction by paying the points with a separate check. Don't allow the bank to deduct the points from the mortgage. Suppose, for instance, you borrow $60,000 and owe 4 points on the loan, or $2400. Don't accept a check from the bank for $57,600 ($60,000 less the $2400 payment of points). Instead, ask for payment of the full mortgage amount, and then hand over your own check for $2400.

Another sizable expense in buying a home is closing costs. These are one-time expenses which include the cost of a title search, title insurance, surveying fees, attorney's fees, mortgage recording tax, and many other smaller bills. Closing costs can total as much as 5 percent of the value of the home you're buying. Before you buy, you should receive from the lending institution a good faith estimate of what your closing costs will be.

Up to this point, we've been concentrating on the most common type of mortgage loan—the "first mortgage," normally taken out to make home purchase possible. However, many homeowners who already have mortgages are now taking advantage of the equity they have built up in their homes by borrowing against that equity. These loans are called *second mortgages* or *home equity loans*.

Homeowners often find second mortgages a convenient source of needed cash. Many banks will lend you up to 75 percent of the equity of your home—that is, the value of your home less the unpaid balance of your mortgage—without requiring lengthy loan applications or long waits for approval. After you take out a second mortgage, you will have to make two monthly loan repayments (one for the original mortgage and one for the second mortgage) to retain your ownership of a single piece of property.

Like first mortgages, second mortgages have varying terms. When a fixed interest rate is charged, the term is usually 15 years or less; when the interest rate is variable, the term may be up to 30 years. The payback period on a second mortgage is often shorter than on a first mortgage. In addition, you may be charged 1 or more extra points for a second mortgage loan. The reason is that the risk to the lender is greater on a second mortgage. If you should be unable to repay your mortgage loans, the holder of the first mortgage has the first claim on the property. The first mortgagor will receive the title to the house and will probably sell it to recoup the loss. Only after the claims of the first mortgagor have been settled will the holder of the second mortgage receive any money.

Within the limits of sensible debt management, it may be advantageous to take out a second mortgage when you need money for some special purpose—educating your children, for example, or taking advantage of a really good investment opportunity. Of course, the additional interest charges you pay will be tax-deductible, somewhat lowering the final cost of the loan. However, this tax deduction may be affected in the near future because of proposed tax reforms. And one word of caution: When seeking a second mortgage, be sure that the contract does not allow the bank to charge you a penalty for early repayment of the loan. Otherwise, if you need or want to sell your home within a few years, you'll lose out when it comes time to settle your mortgage debt.

Municipal Bonds

••

A tax-free investment available in a wide variety of forms to fit almost any investment plan, but ask questions about safety and terms before you buy

Today, few local or state governments can afford to spend the vast sums of money needed to build schools, roads, water and sewer facilities, and other public works. Some towns, cities, and counties are finding it difficult even to meet their day-to-day operating expenses. But these social needs won't just go away. In order to meet them, communities borrow money from citizens and institutions by issuing debt obligations for purchase by investors. These obligations are known as *municipal bonds.*

For the investor, the most important advantage of municipal bonds is the fact that they earn income which is tax-free at the federal level. If you live in the state in which the bonds are issued, they are usually free from state and local income taxes as well. If you're in a high tax bracket, the tax savings can be substantial, but even those whose tax rates are relatively modest should look closely at municipal bonds as a possible investment.

There are over 40,000 different governmental units and agencies currently issuing municipal bonds. They include states, cities, towns, counties, and such agencies as port authorities, highway departments, and housing authorities. Among the varieties of municipal bonds commonly available are the following:

1. **General Obligation (GO) Bonds:** These are backed by the full faith and credit of the issuing agency. Interest payments on GO bonds are supported by the taxing authority of the state or city government. GO bonds are generally considered the safest form of municipal bonds.

2. **Revenue Bonds:** These are usually issued by a government agency or commission which has been charged with operating a self-supporting project, such as a highway or bridge. The money raised through the sale of revenue bonds goes to finance the project, and the income realized from the completed project is used to pay the interest and principal on the bonds. However, if the project earns insufficient income, bondholders may be left holding the bag; the taxpayers of the community are not responsible. Therefore, your risk is greater in buying revenue bonds.

3. **Moral Obligation Bonds or Agency Bonds:** Like revenue bonds, these are issued to finance particular projects—housing projects, public universities, hospitals, and the like. Unlike revenue bonds, the issuing of moral obligation bonds is considered to place the state legislature or local government under a moral obligation to allocate tax monies for the payment of interest and principal should the project fail to generate the necessary income.

General obligation bonds usually pay a slightly lower

rate of interest than either revenue or moral obligation bonds. However, they are somewhat safer.

Municipal bonds have long been a favorite investment of the wealthy. In recent years, inflation has driven many middle-income investors into tax brackets once reserved for the well-off. As a result, the tax-exemption benefits of municipal bonds have attracted flocks of middle-income investors. Let's consider some of the advantages of municipal bonds:

Tax Exemption: As already explained, interest paid on municipal bonds is free of federal income tax and sometimes of state and local income taxes as well. Capital gains realized from the sale of municipal bonds are taxable, however.

Safety: Municipal bonds have historically been a highly safe form of investment, as states and cities, with their power of taxation, have normally been able to meet their debt obligations fully. In recent years, this assumption that municipal bonds are a safe investment has been called into question. We'll consider the issue of safety later in this section.

High Collateral Value: It's usually possible to borrow up to 90 percent of the market value of your municipal bonds from such lenders as banks and brokerage houses, since municipal bonds are free of certain restrictions imposed by the Federal Reserve Board on the use of other bonds as collateral.

Diversity: Thousands of different municipal bonds are available to suit the requirements of individual investors.

Marketability: A large nationwide market for municipal bonds exists, making them easy to sell when necessary. However, you should never buy municipal bonds for speculation. Purchase them for the tax-free income they produce and only in anticipation of what you can get *from* them, not *for* them.

Insurance: It's possible to buy insurance for municipal bonds, usually at a cost of less than ½ percent. If the issuing municipality fails to pay interest or principal as promised, the insurer will make good your investment by continuing to pay the interest, and at maturity the principal.

Attractive as these features may be, municipal bonds are not for everyone. For one thing, a fairly sizable investment is needed. A minimum investment of $5000 is usually required, although, as you'll learn later, you may be able to get around this requirement by investing in a unit trust or mutual fund that specializes in municipal bonds. For another, tax-exempt municipal bonds usually carry a lower rate of interest than taxable bonds. If the tax rate you pay is fairly high, your tax savings will more than make up for the lower return, but those near the bottom of the tax rate tables may be better off with another investment.

To determine whether you should invest in municipal bonds, you must figure out the taxable rate of return equivalent to that paid by tax-exempt municipals. For example, suppose you have a marginal income tax rate of 40 percent and you are offered a tax-exempt municipal bond paying 9 percent interest. To find the equivalent taxable rate of return, take the difference between your marginal tax rate and 100 percent and divide this into the interest rate paid by the tax-exempt bond. Since your marginal tax rate is 40 percent, the difference between this and 100 percent is 60 percent. Divide 60 into 9 and you have a

Table 1. Equivalent Tax-Exempt and Taxable Interest Rates

TAX-EXEMPT RATE	TAXABLE RATE BY TAX BRACKET			
	35%	40%	45%	49%
7%	10.8%	11.7%	12.7%	13.7%
8%	12.3%	13.3%	14.5%	15.7%
9%	13.8%	15.0%	16.4%	17.6%
10%	15.4%	16.7%	18.2%	19.6%
11%	16.9%	18.3%	20.0%	21.6%

figure of about 15 percent. Thus a tax-exempt interest rate of 9 percent is approximately equivalent to a taxable interest rate of 15 percent for someone in the 40 percent tax bracket.

Table 1 shows several typical tax-exempt interest rates along with the equivalent taxable rates for investors in various tax brackets.

For example, this table shows that, for an investor in the 45 percent tax bracket, a 9 percent tax-exempt yield is equivalent to a 16.4 percent taxable yield.

As with any investment, risk is a factor to consider in purchasing municipal bonds. Like corporate bonds, municipal bonds are rated by two major independent rating services, Moody's and Standard and Poor's. A triple-A rating is the highest, a C rating the lowest. In general, the lower the rating, the higher the yield. However, it's recommended not to purchase bonds with a rating lower than AA. The slightly higher interest rate you may be offered on the lower-rated bond isn't worth the sacrifice in safety. Also, when financial times are uncertain, investors will look for quality bonds even though they do produce lower yields.

Until recently, municipal bonds were widely considered to be nearly as safe as U.S. government securities. However, the fiscal problems a few years ago of such major municipalities as New York City and Cleveland, Ohio, have made it apparent that bankruptcy is possible for governments as well as private businesses. The failure of the Washington Public Power Supply System (WPPSS) and the default by WPPSS on payment of interest and principal on the bonds it had issued underscored the issue of safety. This doesn't mean that municipal bonds are a risky investment; it does mean that you should take a close look at the risk factor before buying municipals.

One way to virtually eliminate the risk in buying municipal bonds is to buy bonds that carry a third-party guarantee offered by such groups as the Municipal Bond Assurance Corporation (MBAC) or the American Municipal Bond Assurance Corporation (AMBAC). Bonds insured by either of these agencies are sold at a premium price. However, if the issuing agency should fail, the insurer will continue to make timely payments of interest and principal as agreed upon at the time of purchase. In addition, the insurance will add to the liquidity of your investment, since potential buyers appreciate the greater safety of the insured bonds.

Of course, even MBAC or AMBAC insurance will not protect municipal bonds from fluctuations in value. If a bond-issuing agency defaults, although interest and principal payments will continue, the resale value of the bonds will surely drop. However, since most investors buy bonds for the tax-free income they provide and not primarily in hopes of a large growth in the value of the bonds, this is probably not a major issue for you.

How can you evaluate the safety of a particular municipal bond issue before you buy? Of course, the Moody's or

Standard and Poor's rating is your first guideline. Here are some other points to consider in judging the creditworthiness of a bond-issuing agency:

Sources of Income: A state, city, or county in the throes of a serious, long-term economic decline is, of course, a poor investment risk. Watch out for a steadily declining tax base in an area, as indicated by the flight of businesses and individuals to other states or localities. Income from taxation is usually safest when it is derived in more-or-less equal shares from sales and income taxes.

Diversified Local Economy: Beware of investing in a "company town" dominated by a single industry. Weakness in that industry could devastate the area and prevent the local government from honoring its obligations.

Debt Ratio: The lower the ratio of short-term operating debt to the total budget of the issuing agency, the safer the bond. As a rule of thumb, short-term debt should not exceed 10 percent of income.

Cash Reserves: The issuing agency should have a cash reserve or surplus equal to at least 5 percent of total income.

Callability is a significant factor affecting the value of municipal bonds. When a bond is callable, it may be redeemed by the issuing agency prior to the maturity date, usually at a premium over the face value of the bond. When a municipal bond is issued with a call provision, it usually provides for redemption of the bond within 5 to 10 years after issue. Of course, this places a lid on potential profits, which may be a significant loss to you if interest rates decline significantly after the bond is issued. Even the premium paid on redemption—typically about 2 percent—is usually less than the market value of the bond. So, if possible, try to buy bonds that are non-callable.

If you are considering purchasing a previously issued bond which has a call provision, ask your broker to check as to whether it has already been called. At the time a bond is called, the issuer is required to give notice by placing call-back ads in the financial newspapers. However, these ads may easily be overlooked by the bearers of bonds. Therefore, be sure to check on call-backs. Otherwise, when you turn in a bond that has already been called, you may be required to repay any interest erroneously paid on that bond after the call-back date.

Get quotes from several brokers before buying bonds. Prices on previously issued bonds vary greatly from dealer to dealer, as each sets his or her own profit margin individually. There can, at times, be as much as a 2- or 3-point difference between what the broker pays for the bond (known as the "bid price") and what it can sell for (known as the "asked price"). The matter is further complicated by the fact that municipal bonds are not listed on any exchange, making it that much harder to gauge prices. This caveat doesn't apply to new issues; the issuer pays the dealer's markup on those, so that you'll get the best price no matter where you buy.

December is the best month for finding bargains in the municipal bond market. Many investors swap bonds at the end of the year in search of paper losses which will reduce their tax liability for the year. The consequent pressure to sell usually tends to depress bond prices.

One final point of concern for retired persons: Beginning in January 1984 individual retirees with a total modified adjusted gross income greater than $25,000 and couples with an income greater that $32,000 must pay taxes on a portion of their Social Security income. For the purposes of this computation, modified adjusted gross income includes tax-free municipal bond income. This change somewhat diminishes the value of the tax-exempt status of municipal bonds for retired people.

Municipal Bond Trusts and Funds

••

A way for the small investor to own a share of a diversified portfolio of tax-free municipal bonds

If you've been reading about municipal bonds, you realize that they have many advantages: tax-free income, relative safety, diversity, and liquidity. At one time, these benefits were available only to the well-to-do. The minimum bond purchase is usually $5000. Furthermore, any purchase under $25,000 is considered an "odd-lot" amount and will cost you extra brokerage commissions as well as being harder to sell later. Under these conditions, the municipal bond market was strictly a high-priced investor's playground, and the cost of establishing a diversified portfolio of many municipal bonds was extraordinarily high. It was to remedy this situation that the **municipal bond unit trust** and the **municipal bond mutual fund** were developed.

In some ways, the municipal bond unit trust and the municipal bond mutual fund are similar. Both offer a way for the small investor to buy a portion of a diversified selection of municipal bonds for as little as $1000. Both offer investments that are free of federal income taxes and, in some cases, of state and local taxes (if you live in the state in which the bonds were issued). And both pay interest on a monthly basis, unlike the municipal bonds themselves, which pay interest only semiannually.

However, there are many differences between the unit trust and the mutual fund. Let's explore these differences so that you can decide which of the two might be worth considering as an investment for you. (See Table 2 on page 89.)

A municipal bond unit trust is established by a sponsor who purchases a substantial share in at least 10, but more often 20 or more, long-term bond issues, usually with maturities ranging from 10 to 30 years. The bonds bought by the trust are left intact and do not change once they have been purchased. Therefore, the yield of the trust remains the same throughout its life span, which has a predetermined length that ends when the bonds in the portfolio mature. When you buy a share in a unit trust, you are buying a portion of this fixed portfolio, and you can predict just how long your investment will last and how much it will pay each year.

There are many types of unit trusts, and they vary greatly in terms of their length of maturity, degree of risk, tax-exempt status, and yield. The chances are excellent that you can find a trust with the right combination of features for your investment needs. You can buy units in a trust either (directly) from the sponsoring firm or (indirectly) through your broker. It pays to work through your broker, who can offer you trusts assembled not only by his or her own firm but by other companies as well.

Once all the units in a particular trust have been sold, no more can be issued. You can dispose of your units without incurring a penalty or sales charge by asking your broker or the sponsoring firm to redeem them. In most cases, unit trust sponsors constitute a secondary market for their own units, and will guarantee to buy back your units at their current market value. Of course, this may or may not represent the same amount as you originally paid. If interest rates have risen since the trust was assembled, the rate being paid by the trust may no longer be competitive, and the market value of the units will be less than you paid for them. On the other hand, if interest rates have fallen, you may make a profit when you sell back your shares.

In any case, however, buying and selling units in a bond trust always involves a gap between the bid price and the asked price. The bid price is what the broker pays for the bond; the asked price is the price the broker charges the investor for the same bond. The gap between the two is the broker's profit. It averages about 2 percent of the value of the bond.

Because the portfolio of a unit trust is basically fixed, "managing" the trust is very simple. Therefore, a small management fee or no fee is normally charged. However, when you purchase units in the trust, you must pay a commission which ranges from 2 to 5½ percent, depending on the company sponsoring the trust, its length of maturity, and other factors.

A municipal bond mutual fund is something like a money market fund: Its shares are highly liquid and the portfolio of holdings consists of short-term investments which are continually changing. Whereas a unit trust stands pat with its investments, the managers of a bond fund are constantly trading. Thus the fund as a whole never matures but goes on indefinitely buying and selling bonds to take advantage of changes in the marketplace. Unlike unit trusts, which normally invest in bonds with a maturity of up to 30 years, bond funds invest mainly in bonds with a maturity of 3 years or less.

Table 2.   Municipal Bond Trusts and Funds

FACTORS TO CONSIDER	UNIT TRUST	MUTUAL FUND
Yield	Fixed	Varies with market conditions
Life of investment	Ends when bonds mature	Unending; constantly changing portfolio
Average maturity of bonds held	10–30 years	3 years or less
Purchase	Fixed number of units offered	Shares always available for purchase
Disposal	Units sold through brokers like stock	Shares sold back to fund

Participation in a bond fund usually requires an initial investment of $1000. Anytime thereafter you can buy additional shares in the fund. You have the option of receiving a check for your monthly earnings or having them automatically reinvested to purchase additional shares in the fund. Whenever you wish, you can sell your shares back to the fund. However, since the value of the bonds in the fund's portfolio fluctuates over time, you may or may not get back your original investment when you sell your shares.

Unlike a unit trust, a bond fund is actively managed.

Therefore, a management fee is charged, usually about ½ percent annually.

If you're not sure whether a unit trust or a mutual fund is a better investment for you, follow this rule of thumb: The unit trust is a better choice if you are certain that you want to hold onto the investment for at least 5 years. If you think you may need to liquidate your holdings sooner than that—or if you anticipate shifting to other investments fairly frequently—the mutual fund is preferable. Either investment, however, is a good way for the small- to medium-sized investor to get into municipal bonds with a diversified, professionally selected portfolio of holdings.

Mutual Funds

For those who want to take the plunge into the stock market but aren't sure where to start, a mutual fund may be ideal.

The concept of a ***mutual fund*** is a simple one. A large number of investors put their money together in a pool to be managed by knowledgeable investment professionals. The price of a share in the mutual fund is determined by the value of the fund's holdings. As the value of the stocks owned by the fund increases, the share price increases and the investors make a profit; if the value of the stocks decreases, the investors lose. The price of a share in a mutual fund, determined by dividing the net value of the fund's assets by the number of shares outstanding, is usually announced once or twice a day. The mutual fund also earns dividends which may be paid directly to investors or reinvested to buy additional shares in the fund.

Mutual funds are normally created and managed by brokerage houses. As you'll learn, there are many kinds of mutual funds, depending on the types of stocks invested in, the degree of risk involved, the financial goals of the fund, and other factors. In choosing a fund for your own investment, your personal financial status and goals should be taken into account. We'll give some advice on choosing the best mutual fund for your purposes later in this section.

Mutual funds offer 10 important benefits to prospective stock market investors:

1. **Diversification and Risk Control:** Money you invest in a mutual fund is used to buy shares in many different stock issues. This reduces your investment risk, since the failure of one or two companies out of many will not have a devastating effect on your portfolio. It would be impossible for an individual investor to achieve a comparable degree of diversification without having at least $50,000 to invest in a variety of stocks. Another factor which minimizes your risk in a mutual fund: The Investment Company Act of 1940 requires all mutual funds registered with the Securities and Exchange Commission to post a bond ranging from $500,000 to $2,500,000 as a guarantee against embezzlement and fraud. Your investment in a mutual fund is fairly well protected.

2. **Professional Management:** Few investors have the time, energy, or expertise to keep track of all the many factors affecting the stock market, including changes in interest rates and the money supply, new developments in technology, legal and political developments, foreign competition, and so on. Mutual fund companies have the resources to monitor these developments. Most employ staffs of researchers whose sole task is to keep track of business and economic trends that may affect the performance of stocks in the

fund's portfolio. This expertise works to your benefit when you invest in the fund.

3. **Moderate Cost:** Most mutual funds require only a small initial investment. Management fees are usually modest, averaging about ½ percent of your investment amount annually. If you choose a *no-load fund,* you'll pay no sales commission when you invest in the fund. However, you may have to pay an exit charge or redemption fee (sometimes called a "rear-end load") when you withdraw from the fund. This exit charge, usually about 1 percent of your investment amount, is designed to discourage frequent deposits and withdrawals from the fund.

4. **Performance:** On balance, mutual funds have shown better performance than the stock market as a whole; they have earned higher returns in "bull" (or rising) markets and shown smaller losses in "bear" (or declining) markets.

5. **Fund-Swapping Option:** Many investment firms sponsor more than one type of mutual fund. The firms usually allow their investors to move their money from one fund to another by means of a letter or phone call. This is a convenient way to take advantage of changing investment conditions.

6. **Automatic Deposits:** You can usually arrange for automatic investments to be made in your mutual fund account by specifying a dollar amount to be withdrawn from your bank account on a regular basis. This provides a painless way of building up your investment portfolio month by month.

7. **Automatic Reinvestment:** You can have all dividends, interest, and capital gains earned by your investment automatically reinvested in additional shares in the fund, another painless way of keeping your investment growing.

8. **Ease of Withdrawal:** You can usually withdraw your funds by means of a letter authorizing the redemption of shares. You'll normally receive the money within 7 days.

9. **Reduction of Record Keeping:** The fund handles all stock transactions for you, records any changes in your holdings, and provides periodic statements showing all transactions, dividend distributions, reinvestments, and capital gains.

10. **Life Insurance Availability:** You can buy life insurance to cover your investment commitment. If you designate a beneficiary by means of a trust agreement, your invested funds will go directly to the beneficiary upon your death without incurring the costs or delays involved in the probate process.

As you can see, mutual funds offer many outstanding advantages for those wishing to invest in the stock market. As a result, mutual fund investing is probably the most popular way of getting started in stocks.

Depending on your financial circumstances and your investment objectives, there are many types of mutual funds to choose from. Let's consider the features of the most common types of funds.

Common Stock Fund: This fund invests in common stocks issued by corporations. Stock funds are often classified as either *growth funds* (holding riskier stocks that may pay low or no dividends but are expected to rise in value rapidly) or *income funds* (holding low-risk stocks that pay high dividends but rise in value only slowly).

Bond Fund: This type invests in corporate or government bonds. Bond funds fall into several categories. *High-grade* bond funds deal in top-rated bonds with a high degree of safety and modest yields. *Speculative* bond funds deal in somewhat riskier bonds with ratings in the high Bs that often pay higher yields. *Junk* bond funds carry both the greatest degree of risk and the greatest potential yield. And *municipal* bond funds invest in tax-free bonds issued by state and local governments and government agencies.

Balanced Fund: A balanced fund holds shares in a combination of common stocks, preferred stocks, and bonds.

Industry Fund: Such a fund invests in stocks issued by companies in a specific industry: energy stocks, high-technology stocks, public utilities, and so on.

As your investment needs change over time, so do the kinds of funds which are best for you. When you are young, growth funds are usually best. Your financial needs are often modest at this time, and you can afford to take on a higher degree of risk in exchange for maximum growth potential. As you and your family grow older, diversification among various kinds of funds is desirable. Both stock funds and bond funds belong in your portfolio in middle age. When you near retirement age, current income becomes paramount. Bond funds are probably your best choice at this point. And investors of any age who find themselves in a high tax bracket should consider investing in one of the tax-free funds which invest in municipal bonds or other tax-free investments.

Depending on how they are purchased, mutual funds can be classified as either load or no-load funds. Let's look at the difference.

Shares in a load fund are sold through a stockbroker, who charges a sales commission normally running about 8 percent of the purchase price (this is the *load*). This commission, about three-quarters of which is kept by your individual broker, is deducted from your investment amount before any investment is made. If you deposit $10,000 in a mutual fund that charges a load of 8 percent, only $9200 will actually be invested in the fund. Depending on the performance of the fund, it could take several months to a year to recoup the $800 commission. However, if you plan to remain in the fund for a number of years, the initial sales charge will become relatively unimportant over time. An annual management fee of about ½ percent of your investment is usually also charged.

What does your commission fee pay for? Primarily the advice and services offered by your stockbroker. As an investment professional, he or she should help you select the best fund or funds for your purposes and keep you continually informed as to when you should move in or out of a particular instrument. If your broker doesn't provide this kind of expert advice, consider changing brokers; after all, you're paying for it.

No-load funds are usually sold through the mail by means of advertisements in newspapers or magazines. No sales broker is involved. Therefore, no up-front commission must be paid. However, a small service charge (usually about ½ percent of your investment) is levied each year.

No sales advice or investment services are offered with a no-load fund. However, no-load funds have become increasingly popular in recent years as small investors become better informed and more able to manage their own investments. Performance studies have shown virtually no difference in the earnings of load and no-load funds. Therefore, it is strongly advisable to consider a no-load fund when looking at mutual fund investment.

One more point: There's a definite advantage to investing in a fund which is part of a "family of funds." This is a group of mutual funds with differing investment objectives managed by the same company. You will normally be allowed to move your money from one fund to another either by written notification or by telephone. This offers you maximum flexibility with a minimum of paperwork and lost time. It's worth asking about.

Oil and Gas Shelters

••

A high-risk investment that offers immediate tax benefits and potentially high yields—but a choice that's definitely not for the nervous!

It's clear that no matter what developments occur in fields such as synthetic fuels and solar energy, the United States will be dependent on oil and gas for most of its energy requirements for years to come. In an effort to encourage drilling for oil in this country and so increase U.S. energy independence, the federal government has enacted laws offering tax advantages to investors who put their money into oil and gas partnerships. These are the famous *oil and gas shelters* which have benefited so many wealthy investors in recent years. If you're in a high tax bracket—say, the 40 percent level or higher—you may want to consider investing some of your money in an oil or gas shelter. But be forewarned: Although the potential rewards are great, the risk is high.

Most oil and natural gas deposits in this country are discovered and developed by independent operators. They rely on money from outside investors, like yourself, and usually fund their operations through limited partnerships. In this business structure, the operator is known as the *general partner.* Shares in the partnership are sold to investors who become *limited partners.* Their liability is limited to the amount they've invested; all the work is done by the general partner.

An oil and gas partnership engages in several operations: finding and leasing acreage considered likely to contain oil or natural gas deposits; drilling the wells; producing the oil or gas; and selling it to pipeline companies or refineries. Only about 25 percent of exploratory drilling programs actually discover oil or gas, so the investment is highly speculative. However, today's high oil and gas prices mean that the discovery of even one productive well can produce high income for many years to come. A partnership will normally drill a number of wells in order to maximize the chance of discovering a productive well.

Initial investment in an oil and gas partnership is normally for $5000 to $10,000. It's a good idea to spread your oil and gas shelter money around in several companies, so it's even better to start with $20,000 or more to invest. Obviously, the small investor will probably want to stay away from oil and gas shelters. However, those who can afford them will find that oil and gas shelters can offer substantial tax benefits. Here's how it works:

First, intangible drilling costs, which include costs for wages, supplies, hauling, repairs, and so on, may be deducted from income as business expenses in the year they are incurred. Intangible drilling costs often account for as much as 70 percent of a limited partner's investment.

Next, equipment costs, including the cost of machinery, pumping units, tubing, and so on, are deducted from income according to a 5-year depreciation schedule. Equipment costs also qualify for a 10 percent investment tax credit. This is even better than a deduction, since every dollar of tax credit reduces your tax liability by a dollar.

Then the so-called depletion allowance reduces gross income from oil and gas wells by 15 percent annually. This means that you will not be liable for tax on 15 percent of the annual gross income from your oil and gas investment.

Finally, if the wells owned by the partnership are held long enough, you may incur taxable long-term capital gains when they are sold. However, intangible drilling costs and investment tax credits may be subject to "recapture." This means that a portion of the realized gain on the sale of the wells will be reported as ordinary income for tax purposes, rather than as capital gain.

This summary of the tax benefits of oil and gas shelters should show you several things. First, a sizable portion of the money you invest would otherwise have been paid in income taxes. Therefore, in a sense, you're investing some of the federal government's money as well as your own— but the profits, if any, will be yours alone. Second, the tax benefits involved are fairly complex. You'll probably want to seek the advice of a professional tax adviser before investing in an oil and gas shelter.

If you're considering an oil and gas shelter for your investment portfolio, pay attention to four important factors which will affect the safety of your investment:

1. **Diversification:** The more wells to be drilled under a particular program, the greater the chance of a successful strike and the more likely you are to make a profit on your investment.

2. **Sponsor's Past Performance:** Study the operator's history. A strong past record would include success in 25 percent or more of exploratory programs (that is, drilling programs in new, unexplored areas) and 80 percent or more of developmental programs (that is, drilling programs in areas that were

already producing oil or gas). A record of poor past performance should be a warning to you.

3. **Offering Fees:** The normal range for these fees is between 8 and 12 percent of the investment amount. If fees are too high, the amount of capital available for drilling purposes will be too low.

4. **Risk and Profit Sharing:** It's a good sign if the operator is willing to commit his or her own funds to the project. Ask about this. Also determine how profits will be divided between the operator and the limited partners in the event oil or gas is found.

Oil and gas partnerships are a good tax shelter for those who are willing and able to incur substantial risks with their investment. They may create large first-year write-offs and reduce your effective tax rate by as much as a third or more, and, if successful, can provide income in the 15 percent range annually for a decade or longer. But be sure you know what you're getting into before you sink your funds into oil and gas wells. There's a good chance you'll come up dry.

Public Utilities

For the conservative investor, utility stocks offer a unique combination of stability, safety, and the potential for capital gains.

Public utilities occupy an unusual place in the national economy. Like other private industries, utilities sell shares to stockholders and seek to operate at a profit. However, unlike other businesses, a utility is usually granted monopoly status by the government in exchange for regulation of its prices and services. Thus a public utility normally operates without the outside pressure generated by competition. Historically, this has made investing in utility stocks an unusually safe form of investment. Since utilities provide services generally regarded as essential—water supply, electricity, gas, rail or bus transportation, and the like—they are virtually guaranteed a supply of customers and rarely run into serious financial difficulties.

However, the 1970s were a difficult time for public utilities. Several forces converged to make this so. Inflation soared, increasing costs for all businesses and putting a special squeeze on utilities, whose customer rates are regulated by government. Federal, state, and local regulations hampering utility operations were put into effect. A prime example is in the electrical energy field, where concern over safety and opposition by environmental activists have slowed or halted the construction of nuclear power plants and added greatly to their building and operating costs—this despite the widely conceded efficiency and economy of nuclear power. Factors such as these reduced the profitability of utilities during the 1970s and soured many investors on utility stocks.

In order to help the utilities regain investor confidence, in 1981 Congress established a partial income tax shelter for utility investors. Under this shelter, an investor who bought shares in most large utilities and arranged to have the dividends automatically reinvested in utility stock could deduct from taxable income up to $750 of the reinvested dividends ($1500 for a married couple). The dividends remained tax-free until the stock purchased with them was sold, and if they were held for more than 6 months, the earnings were taxed upon sale as long-term capital gains, rather than as ordinary income. This tax-shelter plan had helped strengthen the investment picture for public utilities but was terminated at the end of 1985.

Other recent developments have added to the attractiveness of utility stocks in the mid-1980s:

- The slowdown in inflation has helped control the growth of utility operating expenses, alleviating the cash flow problems which plagued utilities in the 1970s.

- The growth in demand for electrical power has slowed, reducing the need for new plant construction and the costly outside financing this entails.

- As utilities complete major projects begun in the past decade, they are not committing themselves to new ones, thus improving their return on equity.

- Governmental regulators in most states have begun to look more favorably on utilities and their need to make a reasonable profit within the limits of their privileged monopoly status.

As a result of these and other conditions, utility stocks are again an attractive investment option. Dividends from utilities are currently averaging about 10 percent of the price per share, a higher yield than that offered by, for example, money market funds.

If you're considering buying stock in a particular utility, there are certain points to check which will help you determine how sound an investment it is:

Rate of Return: Naturally, the higher this figure, the better. For comparison purposes, note how the rate of return is derived. This may affect the meaning of the listed percentage. For example, a 10 percent rate of return on a given plant based on its fair market value could be equivalent to a rate of 12 percent or more based on the plant's original cost.

Diversification: It's best if the main business of the utility is operated as a separate corporate entity, with new divisions formed to handle such operations as exploration, development, and so on.

Depreciation: Depreciation at a rate of at least 3 percent should be claimed for federal income tax purposes.

If you're interested in investing in utility stocks but want the benefits of diversification, consider the *tax-managed fund* as an alternative. The tax-managed fund is like any mutual fund investing in stocks; when you buy a share, you are buying part of the portfolio of stocks held by the fund, and you will participate in any profits and losses incurred. However, unlike the ordinary mutual fund, the tax-managed fund makes no distributions to shareholders. Instead, it reinvests all dividends and capital gains in additional stock holdings. Investors make money only when they sell their shares of the fund, which will have increased in value as a result of the reinvestments. Naturally, it's best to hold onto your shares in a tax-managed fund for more than 6 months in order to take advantage of the lower tax rate on long-term capital gains.

Tax-managed funds hold many utility stocks in their portfolios and, in effect, shelter the high dividends they earn from federal taxes. This is because the tax-managed fund operates as a corporation and so pays no tax on 85 percent of its income. The remaining 15 percent can be deducted as business expenses. Thus a tax-managed fund is an attractive way of buying utility stocks, especially for the investor in a high income tax bracket.

As you can see, for the right investor, public utility stocks offer the best of both worlds. They represent a safe choice for the conservative investor, since they enjoy a governmentally sponsored monopoly status and profits which are in large measure protected by government regulation. At the same time, they offer a potential for capital gains, especially when purchased through a tax-managed fund. If you, like many investors, turned away from utility stocks during the 1970s, now is a good time to take a long second look.

Real Estate

Fortunes have been made—and lost—through real estate investments. Be sure you know the property and its value in detail before you sign on the dotted line.

In general, land will always be a sound investment, simply because the amount of land now in existence can never be increased. Therefore, as the population of the world grows, so will demand for land. So the value of *real estate,* under most circumstances, is likely to continue to grow. Furthermore, when you buy real estate for use as rental property, it can benefit you in at least three ways: It provides current income; it provides tax benefits through business expense deductions and depreciation; and, if you like, it can provide a place to live when you retire.

Let's consider first the tax benefits that result from offering property you own for rental purposes. First, any expenses you incur in operating the rental property are deductible from your income as business expenses. These might include repair and maintenance of the house or other property, interest payments on a mortgage, and an occasional trip to inspect the property if it is outside your own residential area.

Second, depreciation can be deducted from your income as well. This is the annual decline in value of any property which results from its increasing age. Depreciation is determined according to a fixed schedule depending on the nature of the property; a house, for example, is usually assumed to have a depreciable life of 20 years, so that you can deduct from your income a specified percentage of the value of the house each year over a 20-year period. This is a noncash deduction, since you are not actually paying out any money, yet you reap tax benefits just as if you were.

Interestingly, real estate values usually increase each year, rather than decrease. Therefore, you benefit twice: The actual resale value of your real property will generally grow, while you get a tax deduction because of the theoretical decrease in the value of your property over time.

Real estate, then, offers decided advantages to the canny investor. But like any other investment, it carries risks as well. The greatest is the risk of buying a property whose rental or resale value is minimal. It has been said that the three most important rules of real estate investment are location, location, and location, and that advice is pretty sound. There's no substitute for knowing the property and its actual value well. Never buy property you haven't personally visited and inspected. Photos or videotapes shown by an agent are no substitute; you'll never see the drawbacks of the property in that way. There are plenty of places in the world where no one is living and where no one will ever want to live. If you buy one of them, your chance of renting or selling the property is small, and mortgage payments, taxes, and other expenses will still have to be met. So above all, make sure you know the property before you buy.

Aside from this fundamental principle, there are other

important rules you should know before you invest in real estate:

- Never buy property solely for its depreciation value. If a piece of real estate isn't a good investment in its own right, its tax benefits will not make it worthwhile.

- Don't buy commercial property if you're a beginner in real estate investing. Single homes and small apartment houses are safer investments and steadier sources of income.

- Buy property within your own community, where you know property values and can anticipate trends. Your chance of success in the real estate field decreases with distance from your home base.

- Use as little cash as possible when buying real estate for investment purposes. Make a small down payment, and take out the largest mortgage you can afford.

- Never sign an agreement you don't fully understand. Hidden loopholes can be costly. For example, some installment sale contracts withhold ownership until the property is fully paid for. This may take years, and you run the risk of losing everything if illness or unforeseen financial reversals interrupt your payments.

- Don't invest in real estate unless you can reasonably foresee an annual profit from your investment, after deducting expenses and taxes, of at least 15 percent. The property itself should have a reasonable prospect for appreciation of about 10 percent annually.

- When offering property for rental, be sure your interests as landlord are fully protected. Have a law-

yer draw up a lease outlining the agreement between you and your tenant.

- Remember that renting can mean headaches for
  you as a landlord. The property must be maintained
  according to health and safety standards set by local
  governments, and complaints from tenants can be
  annoying. You might consider having a professional
  manager operate your property, but his or her fee,
  ranging from 6 to 10 percent of the rent, will cut
  heavily into your profit.

There is one effective way of avoiding many of the
problems of managing rental property while enjoying the
tax benefits: Rent a home you own to relatives, such as
your parents. This can be beneficial to both parties and
will eliminate the worries of dealing with strangers for
tenants (unless, of course, you have parents who are especially grouchy). Note that, until 1981, the Internal Revenue Service did not allow any tax deduction for renting
property to close relatives. However, Congress eliminated
the restriction in that year.

If you're interested in real estate investment but somewhat hesitant to get involved directly, consider a ***real estate
investment trust (REIT)***. Like a mutual fund a REIT pools
money from many investors who buy shares in the trust's
portfolio. However, rather than investing in stocks or
bonds, a REIT invests in real estate. REIT investments fall
into three categories:

1. Equity, or ownership of real estate properties,
   whether commercial, industrial, or residential
2. Long- or intermediate-term mortgages
3. Short-term loans for real estate construction and
   development

In July 1985 the Rockefeller family mortgaged New York City's famous Rockefeller Center for over $1 billion by setting up a REIT. Large investors like the Rockefellers can establish a REIT that takes over their own real estate. This is known as "cashing out."

REIT investments may be very conservative or highly speculative, depending upon the policy set by the management of the trust. You'll want to make sure that the objectives of the trust match your own investment plans before you get involved.

REITs have a number of advantages for investors. They allow small investors to participate in real estate investments that would otherwise be unavailable. Shares in a REIT are generally fairly liquid and can normally be sold at or near their full value. By federal regulation, over 90 percent of the earnings of a REIT must be distributed annually to shareholders, and these earnings are not subject to corporate income tax. Long-term capital gains earned by the trust are distributed to shareholders and taxed at the long-term rates.

Naturally, REITs have their disadvantages as well. Management and operating fees are charged, which reduce the net earnings of the trust and the amount of investor distributions as well. The tax benefits normally associated with real estate ownership—including deductions for depreciation, interest, and maintenance costs—are absorbed by the trust, rather than passed on to individual investors. And, in some cases, REITs trade only thinly, making them difficult to dispose of quickly.

If you're considering becoming a shareholder in a REIT, ask the following key questions:

- Who is managing the properties to be purchased by the REIT? What track record can the managers show in managing similar properties?

- What acquisition fees, if any, will be charged?
- What percentage of the capital raised by the REIT will be retained by the originator as profit?

You should have satisfactory answers to these questions before you put your money into a REIT.

Over the past 2 decades, real estate values in the United States have soared. Few other investments have shown a comparable rate of growth. If the U.S. economy continues to prosper, real estate will continue to benefit. As long as you know what you're buying, the chances are that you can do very well by investing in real estate.

The Salary
Reduction Plan:
401(k) Plan

●●

A new type of profit-sharing plan that allows you to shelter a big chunk of your salary from taxes—with the help of your employer

An increasingly popular way of saving for retirement is the ***401(k) plan,*** named after the tax law provision that makes it possible. Also known as the "deferred salary" or "salary reduction plan," the 401(k) plan allows an employee to set aside part of his or her salary into a tax-sheltered account which grows tax-free until after retirement. Since you don't have to pay current income tax on the money you deposit in your 401(k) account, the plan is something like an individual retirement account (IRA). However, unlike an IRA, a 401(k) plan must be set up by your employer. And most employers who establish 401(k) plans make matching contributions on behalf of their employees—a wonderful benefit for you, if you're on the receiving end!

The 401(k) account differs from an IRA in other ways too. Whereas the limit on contributions to an IRA is $2000 per year, you and your employers can make a combined investment contribution of up to $30,000 per year or 25 percent of your salary (whichever is less) into your 401(k) account. With an IRA, you indicate the size of your contribution as a deduction on your federal income tax return. With a 401(k), this is not necessary. Your contribution is deducted from the income reported on your W-2 form, and therefore is automatically excluded from federal and state income taxes. However, you do have to pay Social Security taxes on the amount of your contribution.

Most 401(k) plans provide for employee contributions of 6 to 10 percent of salary, with equal amounts contributed by the employer. An employee earning $32,000 annually who participated in a 401(k) plan allowing an 8 percent salary deferral would only receive (and pay income tax on) $29,440 in salary payments; the rest would be set aside until retirement. However, the full $32,000 would be subject to Social Security tax.

At the time the 401(k) plan is established by the employer, a specific investment program is set up. The employer usually chooses an investment firm to manage the accounts, and a range of possible investment options is offered. These choices are usually more restricted than they would be with an IRA. Whereas almost any investment vehicle is permissible with an IRA, only a handful of options are allowed with a 401(k): a fixed-interest annuity, a mutual fund investing in stocks, a money market fund, and, perhaps, stock in the company itself. You can opt to put all your contributions into one or another investment vehicle, or you can split your contributions among two or more choices.

If you leave the company, you can withdraw your 401(k) savings and, if you like, you can keep the money. However, it becomes subject to income taxes during that year. You can avoid this by rolling the money over into an IRA. You are also eligible to withdraw your 401(k) money at any time without having to pay a penalty if you suffer a financial hardship. At the present time, the Internal Revenue Service (IRS) has been interpreting the "hardship" provision fairly liberally. You would qualify for the hardship clause if you become disabled or incur sizable medical bills not reimbursed by insurance. You may also be able to use your 401(k) funds for such major expenses as your children's college tuition or the down payment on a new home. However, you may want to seek the advice of an accountant or tax attorney before you go ahead; IRS rulings on what constitutes "hardship" are likely to change from time to time.

Once you reach age 59½, the money in your 401(k) account is yours to do with as you please. Of course, it is taxable when you withdraw it. However, your income will probably be lower after you retire, and so will your tax bracket. And the 401(k) account has another major advantage over the IRA when withdrawal time comes. If you withdraw your IRA funds in a lump sum, you must suffer a big tax bite during that year. However, if you withdraw your 401(k) funds in a lump sum, you can use *10-year forward averaging* to spread out and reduce the tax payments. This means that the withdrawal is taxed as if you'd received only one-tenth of the money each year for a period of 10 years. The savings this option allows you can be quite significant.

As you can see, the 401(k) plan is a very attractive investment option for employees—especially since the usual employer matching-contribution program in effect doubles your annual savings at no cost to you. More and more employers are offering 401(k) plans as part of their fringe benefit packages and to supplement existing pension plans. In some regions, over half of all companies are currently offering or plan to offer 401(k) plans. If your employer is among those making this investment option available, take advantage of it. And if you can afford to contribute to both a 401(k) account and an IRA, do that too. You'll benefit right now as well as when you retire.

Stocks

●●●

Do you have strong nerves, native shrewdness, and a good sense of timing? If so, you may be ready to join the millions of Americans who've invested money—as well as time and emotion—in playing the stock market.

There's no doubt that investing in the stock market can be one of the most exciting ways of making money. Nothing quite compares with the thrill of seeing the little-known stock you picked become a hot property, perhaps doubling in price—and then doubling again and again. But as with any investment, the potential risks are equal to the rewards. The middle-income investor who wants to play the market owes it to himself or herself to become fully informed before getting involved. This chapter should be only the beginning of a continuing process of education for anyone interested in becoming a successful stock market investor.

A share of stock represents a unit of ownership in a corporation. When you buy stock, you are becoming a part-owner of the business. Therefore, you benefit from any increase in the value of the corporation, and you suffer when the corporation performs badly. You're also entitled to share in the profits earned by the corporation.

Stocks are bought and sold in marketplaces known as **stock exchanges**. The exchange itself does not buy or sell stock, nor does it set the price of stock; the exchange is simply a forum in which individuals and institutions may trade in stocks. Stock exchanges play a vital role in a capitalist economy. They provide a way for individuals to purchase shares in thousands of businesses, and they provide businesses with an important source of capital for expansion, growth, research, and development.

There are two types of stock exchanges: *organized* and *unorganized*.

There are some 14 organized stock exchanges currently operating in the United States, of which the New York Stock Exchange (NYSE) is both the best known and the largest (over 1300 members). Only members may trade shares in a stock exchange, and only individuals may become members, although a member may be a partner or an officer in a brokerage firm (known as a "member firm"). To become a member, you must buy a membership, or "seat," from another member or from an estate. The price of a seat varies greatly, depending on the volume of business being transacted. A seat on the NYSE has sold for as little as $17,000 (in 1942) and as much as $625,000 (in 1929—just before the great crash).

Most brokerage firms own seats on an exchange, with one of the firm's officers designated as a member. In their role as brokers, members carry out clients' orders to buy or sell securities on the floor of the exchange. In communication with other exchange members, brokers can carry out buy-and-sell transactions right on the exchange floor. Current sale prices on each stock being traded are constantly updated and made available to all members. Thus the exchange operates as a kind of auction market for the trading of securities.

Here's what happens when an investor decides to buy or sell a particular stock:

First, an account executive at the brokerage house receives the buy or sell order. The order may take any of several forms:

Round Lot: An order to buy or sell 100 shares, considered the standard trading unit

Odd Lot: An order to buy or sell fewer than 100 shares

Market: An order to buy or sell at the best available price

Limit: An order to buy or sell at a specified price

Stop: An order designed to protect profits or limit losses by calling for sale of stock when its price falls to a specified level

Good till Canceled (GTC): An order that remains open until it is executed or canceled by the investor

Second, after the order is received, it is sent by teletype to the floor of the stock exchange. The brokerage firm's floor broker receives the order and executes it at the appropriate trading post. Confirmation of the transaction is teletyped back to the account executive at the local office, who notifies the investor. Remarkably, the entire process may take as little as 2 or 3 minutes.

Not all stocks are traded on 1 of the 14 organized exchanges. Those that are not are traded "over the counter" in the so-called unorganized exchange. Not a physical place, the unorganized exchange consists of thousands of brokers and dealers who trade in about 50,000 different unlisted stocks through telephone or telegraph communication. A computer system, known as the National Association of Security Dealers Automated Quotation system (NASDAQ), is used to provide instant bid and asked prices on stocks.

In the over-the-counter market, transactions are negotiated privately, rather than on an auction basis. An investor wishing to purchase a particular unlisted security consults a broker, who contacts other brokers dealing in that stock. The broker offering the stock for sale at the lowest price receives the offer.

Prices of over-the-counter stocks are quoted as both *bid* and *asked* prices. The bid price is the final price offered by a buyer, while the asked price is the final price requested by a seller. Trades are normally made when the bid and asked prices approach one another.

There are two kinds of stocks: *common* and *preferred*.

A share of common stock represents a unit of ownership, or "equity," in the issuing corporation. Each share of common stock usually bears a *par value*, which is a more-or-less arbitrary value established in the corporation's charter and bearing little relation to the stock's actual market value. The market value is influenced by many factors, including the corporation's potential earning power, its financial condition, its earnings record, its record for paying dividends, and general business conditions.

Ownership of a share of common stock carries certain privileges:

1. A share in earnings: Each year, the board of directors of the corporation meets to determine the amount of the corporation's earnings that will be distributed to stockholders. This distribution, known as the *dividend*, will vary depending on the company's current profitability. It may be omitted altogether if the company is earning no current

profits or if the board elects to plow back profits into growth.

2. A share in control: Holders of common stock have the right to vote on matters of corporate policy on the basis of one vote per share held. However, the small investor with only a few shares of stock has little or no practical influence on corporate decisions.

3. A claim on assets: In the event of the company's liquidation, holders of common stock have the right to share in the firm's assets after all debts and prior claims have been satisfied.

There are four main categories of common stocks, each of which is best for a particular investment strategy and purpose:

1. **Blue-Chip Stocks:** High-grade, or blue-chip, stocks are issued by well-established corporations with many years of proven success, earnings growth, and consistent dividend payments. Blue-chip stocks tend to be relatively high priced and offer a relatively low income yield. However, they are a very safe investment.

2. **Income Stocks:** These pay a higher-than-average return on investment. They are generally issued by firms in stable businesses which have no need to reinvest a large percentage of profits each year.

3. **Growth Stocks:** Issued by firms expected to grow rapidly during the years to come, growth stocks have a current income that is often low, since the company plows back most earnings into research and expansion. However, the value of the stock

may rise quickly if the company performs up to expectations.

4. **Speculative Stocks:** These are backed by no proven corporate track record or lengthy dividend history. Stocks issued by little-known companies or newly formed corporations, high-flying "glamour" stocks issued by companies in new business areas, and low-priced "penny stocks" may all be considered speculative stocks. As with any speculative investment, there is a possibility of tremendous profit—but a substantial risk of losing all as well.

Preferred stock, like common stock, represents ownership of a share in the corporation. However, holders of preferred stock have a prior claim on the company's earnings as compared with holders of common stock; hence the name "preferred stock." Similarly, holders of preferred stock have a prior claim on the company's assets in the event of liquidation.

Preferred stock also has certain distinctive features related to dividend payments. A fixed, prespecified annual dividend is usually paid for each share of preferred stock. This fixed dividend may be expressed in dollars (for example, $10 per share) or as a percentage of the stock's par value. It must be paid before dividends are issued to holders of common stock.

However, preferred stock dividends are not considered a debt of the corporation—unlike, for example, the interest due on corporate bonds—because the firm is not obligated to meet its dividend payments. If the corporation is losing money, the board of directors may decide to withhold the dividend payment for a given year. To protect stockholders against undue losses, most preferred stock is issued with a *cumulative* feature. If a dividend is not paid on cumulative preferred stock, the amount is carried over to the following period, and both dividends must be paid before holders of common stock can receive any dividend.

Some preferred stocks are *convertible*. This means that shares of preferred stock can be exchanged for shares of common stock issued by the same company. Prices of convertible preferred stocks tend to vary more than those of other preferred stocks, since they are affected by changes in the prices of the corresponding common stocks.

Unlike common stock, preferred stock carries no voting privileges. Most of the stock issued in the United States is of the common, rather than preferred, variety.

Now that you know the basic characteristics of the different kinds of stocks, let's take a look at some of the things you should know to get started in stock market investing.

Any investor's most important tool is *information*: information about stock prices, movement in the market, and likely future business trends. Without plenty of sound information, investment decisions are pure guesswork. The first place to look for information about any stock is the financial pages of your newspaper, and the best place to start is with the columns listing the current stock prices on one or more of the major organized exchanges. Figure 2 provides an explanation of the information you'll find in those columns and what it means for you as a prospective investor.

The sample in Figure 2 shows a typical listing for a stock traded on one of the major exchanges. Newspapers can list only a small fraction of the thousands of stocks traded over the counter. Therefore, a phone call to your broker is a must if you are interested in the day's activity in a particular over-the-counter (OTC) stock. Newspaper

High (1)	Low (1)	Stock (2)	Div (3)	P/E (4)	100s (5)	High (6)	Low (7)	Last (8)	Change (9)
44	16	XYZ	.95	7	33	35¼	34	35	+½

1. **High** and **Low:** These are the highest and lowest prices paid for the stock during the previous year (over 52 weeks). This entry shows that the highest price paid for XYZ stock during the previous year was $44 per share; the lowest price, $16 per share.

2. **Stock:** Stocks are listed alphabetically by an abbreviated form of the corporate name.

3. **Dividend:** The rate of annual dividend is shown; it is generally an estimate based on the previous quarterly or semiannual payment. This entry shows that XYZ is paying an annual dividend of 95 cents per share.

4. **Price/Earnings Ratio:** This is the ratio of the market price of the stock to the annual earnings of the company per share of stock. As you'll learn later, this is an important indicator of corporate success and investor confidence.

5. **Shares Traded:** This is the number of shares sold for the day, expressed in hundreds. In the example shown, 3300 shares of XYZ stock were traded. The figure does not include odd-lot sales. Note: if the number in this column is preceded by a "z," it signifies the actual number of shares traded, not hundreds.

6. and 7. **High** and **Low:** These are the highest and lowest prices paid for XYZ stock during the trading session (that is, the business day). The highest price paid for XYZ stock was $35.25 per share; the lowest price, $34 per share. Stock prices are shown in dollars and fractions of dollars, ranging from ⅛ to ⅞.

8. **Closing Price:** The final price of XYZ stock for the day. In this case, it was $35 per share.

9. **Change:** The difference between the closing price of the stock for this session and the closing price for the previous session. Since XYZ stock closed at $35 per share, up ½ (or 50 cents) from the previous close, yesterday's closing price would have been $34.50.

Figure 2.   Sample Stock Listing

Stock	Bid	Asked	Bid Change
DESC	7¼	8¼	+¾

Stock: The abbreviated name of the issuing company.

Bid: This is the price dealers are willing to buy the stock at; in this case, $7.25 per share.

Asked: This is the price dealers are willing to sell the stock at; it is always higher than the bid price. In this case, it is $8.25 per share.

Bid Change: This is the difference between the bid price today and the bid price at the close of the previous day. Since today's bid price is up ¾ from the previous day's close, the bid price yesterday was $6.50 per share.

Figure 3.   Sample OTC Stock Listing

listings for OTC stocks are simpler than those for stocks traded on a major exchange (see Figure 3).

The information in a newspaper listing is a useful place to start in analyzing the value of a particular stock. However, it's only a starting place. Facts derived from the annual report issued by a corporation, newspaper and magazine articles about the business, stock market newsletters and columnists' comments, and the advice of your broker can all be helpful. In particular, there are certain statistics that are widely available for any listed stock which can tell you a good deal about the investment prospects for that stock. Let's take a look at them.

1. **Earnings per Share:** The current earnings-per-share figure is one basic measure of the success of a corporation. It is computed by taking the corporation's net profit after taxes, subtracting any prefer-

red stock dividends, and dividing the remainder by the number of outstanding shares of common stock. For example, suppose XYZ Corporation earned a net profit of $4,300,000 last year, paid a dividend on preferred stock of $300,000, and has 800,000 outstanding shares of common stock. The earnings per share for XYZ Corporation is $5:

$4,300,000	Net profit after taxes
− 300,000	Dividend on preferred stock
4,000,000	
÷ 800,000	Outstanding shares of common stock
$5	Earnings per share

2. **Book Value:** This is one measure of the value of the assets of the corporation. It is computed by taking the listed value of the assets, subtracting amounts due to creditors and preferred stockholders, and dividing the remainder by the number of outstanding shares of common stock. To take another simple example, suppose XYZ Corporation owns assets valued at $30 million, has debts totaling $10 million, and has 800,000 shares of common stock outstanding. The book value of XYZ Corporation is $25 per share:

$30,000,000	Assets
−10,000,000	Debts and value of preferred stock
20,000,000	
÷ 800,000	Outstanding shares of common stock
$25	Book value per share

3. **Price/Earnings (P/E) Ratio:** This important index allows you to compare the market price of the

stock to its demonstrated earning power. A low P/E ratio—say, under 7—shows that the company has high earnings relative to the current market price of its stock and suggests that the market has undervalued the stock. The stock is probably a good buy at its current price. Conversely, a high P/E ratio shows that the market expects large future earnings from the company and has therefore driven up the price of the stock. The P/E ratio is computed by dividing the stock's market price by the company's earnings per share. If stock in XYZ Corporation is selling at $35 per share, and the company has earnings of $5 per share, the P/E ratio is 35:5, or 7.

4. **Yield:** This figure offers another indication as to how reasonable the current price of a stock is. It is a percentage determined by dividing the current annual dividend per share by the current market price of a share. If XYZ Corporation is paying an annual dividend of 95 cents per share, and the stock is selling at $35 per share, then the yield is 0.95:35, or about 2.7 percent.

5. **Rate of Return:** The rate of return on a given stock is a measure of the total profit you gain from holding that stock for a specified period of time. Computing the rate of return involves several steps. First, find the total market value of your stock at the end of the period in question. Add to this figure the total amount of dividends earned by the stock during the period. Divide this sum by the total market value of the stock at the start of the period. Subtract 1, and multiply by 100. The resulting figure, expressed as a percentage, is your rate of return for the period.

Here's an example. Suppose you bought 100 shares of XYZ stock at $24 per share. You've held the stock for 1 year. The stock paid a $2 per share dividend during the course of the year. At the end of the year, it has a market value of $25 per share. The rate of return for this stock is 12.5 percent, calculated in this way:

$2500   Market value of stock at end of period
+ 200   Dividend paid during period
―――――
2700
÷2400   Market value of stock at start of period
―――――
1.125

$$1.125 - 1 = 0.125 \times 100 = 12.5 \text{ percent rate of return}$$

Each of these five indicators—earnings per share, book value, price/earnings ratio, yield, and rate of return—is an important factor in judging the value of a stock offering.

When attempting to gauge or predict large-scale trends in stock market values, the Dow Jones Industrial Average is often cited. The most frequently mentioned of four Dow Jones averages (covering industrial stocks, transportation stocks, utility stocks, and a composite average), the Dow Jones Industrial Average is a barometer of stock market trends based on prices of 30 large U.S. corporations listed on the NYSE. Every day, the fluctuations in the prices of these stocks are combined by adding together the prices of the 30 stocks and dividing the result by a factor of 1.359 (used to compensate for complicating factors, such as stock splits and periodic substitutions in the list of stocks used). The 30 stocks currently used (May 1985) in computing the Dow Jones Industrial Average are:

Allied Corporation	Inco Ltd.
Alcoa	IBM
American Brands	International Harvester
American Can	International Paper
American Express	Merck
AT&T	Minnesota Mining
Bethlehem Steel	Owens-Illinois
Chevron	Procter & Gamble
Du Pont	Sears, Roebuck
Eastman Kodak	Texaco
Exxon	Union Carbide
General Electric	U.S. Steel
General Foods	United Technologies
General Motors	Westinghouse
Goodyear	F. W. Woolworth

This is a very stable list, by the way; in the last 4 years, only three of the names on the list have changed and two of the corporations listed—General Electric and American Brands—have been on the list for over 87 years.

The Dow Jones Industrial Average has been widely criticized as an inaccurate reflection of the U.S. economy and the U.S. stock market. The Dow is weighted with older, heavy manufacturing firms and doesn't fully measure the impact of newer high-tech companies. The mathematical method used in calculating the Dow has also been attacked on various technical grounds. Other indexes, such as the Standard & Poor Composite Index, which is based on prices of 500 stocks, have been created to compete with the Dow. Nonetheless, the Dow Jones Industrial Average remains the most popular and influential measurement of the direction and strength of the U.S. stock market.

Like any investment, stocks have distinct advantages and disadvantages. Some of these should have already become apparent. Let's take a systematic look at them. First, the advantages of investing in stocks:

Growth Potential: When a company has the potential for growth in value and earnings, so does its stock. If you pick the right stock or group of stocks, you can profit significantly and relatively quickly. History shows that, as a whole, the stock market has had an upward trend in values, with years of gain outnumbering those of decline by better than 3 to 1.

Liquidity: Stocks traded on the major exchanges can be bought and sold quickly and easily at prices readily ascertained.

Possible Tax Benefits: Growth stocks, which pay low or no dividends so that company profits can be reinvested, provide an effective tax shelter for your profits. As the corporation's value grows, so does the value of your stock, which is a form of tax-deferred income, since no taxes need be paid on these gains until you sell the stock.

Now, the disadvantages:

Risk: There can be no guarantee that you will make money investing in stocks. Companies may fail, stock prices may drop, and you may lose your investment.

Brokerage Commissions: Most investors need the help and advice of a stockbroker when playing the market. However, high broker's commissions can largely erode your profits. Since one fee is charged when you buy your stocks and another when you sell them, you are, in effect, forced to pay twice. If you're an unusually well informed investor, consider one of the growing firms of *discount brokers*, which provide little or no investment counseling but charge greatly reduced commissions when trading your stocks.

Complexity: The stock market is a complicated subject, and the amount of knowledge needed to be consistently successful is tremendous. Investors who lack the patience, time, or skill to inform themselves about the market often buy and sell on impulse, thereby minimizing their profits and maximizing their losses. If you get into the stock market, be prepared to devote the time and work necessary to make intelligent decisions, rather than haphazard ones.

Before we conclude this brief primer on the stock market, let's look at some special topics that apply to certain stock issues.

Stock Dividends: These are extra shares of stock issued to stockholders in place of cash dividends. The size of a stock dividend is expressed in percentage terms; for example, if a company declares a 10 percent stock dividend, it will give each stockholder 10 new shares of stock for every 100 already owned. Stock dividends allow a corporation to conserve much-needed cash. They also allow stockholders to shelter their income from taxes, since stock dividends, unlike cash dividends, need not be declared as income on your tax return. However, a stock dividend which is not justified by company profits tends to dilute the value of the stock. An 8 percent stock dividend should be supported by an 8 percent yield, computed as explained above. If it is not, the shareholder may suffer in the long run.

Stock Splits: A stock split is like a very large stock dividend. When a board of directors votes to split the stock, it divides the outstanding shares of the company's stock into a larger number of shares. The value of the stock is usually divided in the same way. For example, suppose a certain stock is selling at $60 per share. The board of directors votes a 3-for-1 split. Each shareholder receives two additional shares for each share he or she already owns. Each of the three shares is now valued at $20. The purpose of a stock split is to make the stock more attractive to investors, since more people are willing and able to buy the stock at its new, lower price. It often results in an increase in the price of the newly split stock, as new investors become interested in the company. All things being equal, the newly split $20 shares described above may shortly rise in value to $25 or $30.

Stock Rights: A corporation in need of capital may issue stock rights to its shareholders. These are options to purchase additional shares of stock at a discount price; they are usually issued in amounts proportional to the number of shares already owned. For example, a shareholder may be given the right to buy 1 discounted share for every 5 shares he or she owns. Stock rights are usually transferable and are often bought and sold on their own. To determine the value of a stock right, find the difference between the market value of a share of stock and the discounted price. Divide this by the number of shares you must own to receive one stock right, plus 1. The result is the value of each right. For example, suppose the market value of a given stock is $30; rights are issued giving shareholders the option of buying stock at a $26 price; and 5 shares must be owned for every 1 discounted share to be purchased. The value of each right is 67 cents:

$$\frac{30 - 26}{5 + 1} = \frac{4}{6} = 0.67$$

If you're offered stock rights on a company whose stock you own, check with your broker. There's normally an expiration date by which the rights must be exercised. Even if you don't want to exercise them yourself, you may want to sell them.

Stock Warrants: A warrant is an option to buy a specified number of shares of stock at a specified price. Like a stock right, it becomes invalid after a specified date. The price specified by the warrant, called the *exercise price*, is fixed higher than the market price at the time the warrant is sold. Investors buy warrants in the belief that the value of the stock will rise above the exercise price prior to the expiration date. Warrants are a highly speculative investment.

Stock Options and
Commodity Futures

••

For sophisticated investors only: two ways of buying a chance for sizable profits while risking little of your own money

If you've been playing the stock market for some time and think you have a good feeling for how stocks are likely to rise and fall in the near future, you may want to get involved in buying *stock options*. This is an investment technique that's not for the novice but which can be exciting—and profitable—for those who understand its intricacies.

When you buy a stock option, you are not actually buying stock. Instead, you are buying the right to either buy or sell 100 shares of a given stock at a specified price within a certain period of time. An option to buy is known as a *call*; an option to sell is known as a *put*. The specified buying or selling price is known as the *striking price*, and the deadline by which the option must be exercised is known as the *expiration date*.

Here are a couple of simple examples of how stock options work. Suppose you feel the price of AJL stock, currently valued at $70 a share, is about to increase. You might buy a call giving you the right to buy 100 shares of

AJL stock for $70 a share. If you pay $3 a share for this privilege, you have a stake in $7000 worth of stock for only $300 plus broker's commission. Conversely, if you think that the price of AJL stock is due to fall, you might buy a put giving you the right to sell 100 shares of AJL stock at $70 a share. If you pay $2 a share for this privilege, you have a financial stake in the price movement of $7000 worth of shares for just $200 plus commission. In both cases, the idea is to profit from stock price fluctuations without having to purchase the shares themselves.

The price of a stock option is called the *premium*. The premium will vary depending on the length of the option contract (which may be from 30 days to 6 months or longer), the type of stock issue covered, and the general activity of the market.

Let's look at a more detailed example of how buying a stock option can allow you to make a substantial profit while risking very little of your own money.

Suppose MASTCA Corporation is currently selling at 28½ per share. You believe that MASTCA is due for a substantial increase, but you have only $2000 available to invest. If you bought MASTCA stock directly with your $2000, you could buy approximately 70 shares of stock. If you did this and MASTCA increased by 8 points over the next 9 months, you could then sell your 70 shares and make a profit of $560 (less broker's commission).

However, suppose you bought 10 MASTCA call options at a premium of $2 per share instead. Your profit would be much greater. The 10 options, which would cost $2000, would give you the right to buy 1000 MASTCA shares at the current price of 28½. If the stock moves up by the same 8 points, you can, in effect, buy it at 28½, immediately resell it at 36½, and make a total profit of $4500 (less commission), figured as follows:

36½	Selling price
−30	Striking price
6½	Profit
− 2	Cost of option
4½	Net profit per share

Since the 10 options you bought represented 1000 shares, your profit at 4½ per share would total $4500.

As this example shows, call options are for people who expect a stock to go up and are unwilling or unable to commit the full purchase price of the stock. Put options work in just the opposite fashion; you would buy them when you expect the price of a stock to go down.

Options available for purchase appear in the daily financial listings of leading newspapers. Table 3 shows calls available for MASTCA Corporation as of February 1. Assume that the current price is 28½.

Look carefully at Table 3. Although the current price of the stock is 28½, you can buy a call option to buy the stock at 25 with a premium of $5 per share for April expiration, $5.75 per share for July expiration, and $6.50 per share for October expiration. Thus purchasing an April call would cost you $500 for 100 shares and would

Table 3.　Options

Title	CALLS			
	Strike Price	April	July	October
MASTCA	25	5	5¾	6½
	30	1½	1⅞	2
	35	⅛	¼	½

give you the right to buy the stock at $25 per share and resell it at any current price any time prior to the third Friday in April. Therefore, if the stock reaches $30 a share any time before April, you've broken even (since $25 per share plus the $5 premium equals $30). Any price beyond $30 a share will earn you a profit.

Of course, if the price fails to reach $30 before April, you'll lose money on your option, although never more than the $500 you've invested in the option itself. Note, too, that as the striking price on MASTCA options moves higher (to $30 and $35 per share), the option premium falls, since the stock would have to increase that much more in order for you to make a profit.

A put option works like a call option in reverse. With a put option, you have the right to sell shares at a specified price. It is a sound investment when you believe that a stock is due to fall in value.

A classic example of the profit power of a put option occurred on October 18, 1983. On that date, Digital Equipment was selling for about $100 a share, with puts selling at 25 cents a share which gave investors the right to sell the stock at $95 a share by October 21 (just 3 days later).

At midday on October 18, Digital Equipment announced poor earnings performance for the quarter, and the value of the stock dropped to just $79. This gave the put option a value of $16 per share (that is, $95 minus $79) on the same day in which it was selling in the morning for only 25 cents per share. Someone who had made a $1000 investment in the morning would have yielded $64,000 by the afternoon!

But remember—for every lucky investor who bought a put option on Digital Equipment, there was another who sold it. Even worse, there were those who bought call options on Digital Equipment, hoping that it would go up.

If you're an intrepid investor interested in braving the stock options market, here are some basic points to consider before taking the plunge:

- Buy call options in a rising market; buy put options in a falling market.
- Buy options on volatile stocks with a history of rapid price movement.
- Try not to pay a premium of more than $3 per share on a stock selling under 50, and no more than $5 per share on a stock selling over 60.
- Follow your option on a daily basis; like stocks themselves, calls and puts are traded continually and can be traced through newspaper listings.
- The longer the period before the expiration date on your option, the greater your chance for profit. Therefore, go with longer expiration dates, even though they are more costly, and avoid options with less than 2 months to run.
- Remember that all profits earned through options trading are classed as short-term capital gains, which are taxed at the highest rate.
- The greatest advantage of options as an investment is that you know in advance the exact amount you can lose, which is limited by the cost of the option itself. But bear in mind that options are extremely volatile, and should be traded only by investors who understand the risks and requirements and have weighed them carefully against the potential rewards.

Another way of investing in possible future trends of prices without risking much money of your own involves trading in *commodity futures*. If anything, commodity trading is even more speculative than trading in stock options. So read on only if you have money you can afford to risk with no guarantee of profit.

Commodities are traded on about a dozen commodity exchanges in this country, of which the largest is the Chicago Board of Trade. Among the commodities traded are coffee, copper, cotton, heating oil, livestock, orange juice, precious metals, wheat, and sugar. Trading in commodity futures is something like trading in stock options, since it is based on your expectations as to how the price is likely to change in the future. If you believe that the price of a certain commodity—copper, for example—is likely to rise in the near future, you could purchase a copper futures contract. This would allow you to, in effect, buy a large amount of copper at today's prices and sell it later at the higher price.

When you buy a commodity futures contract, you do not take physical possession of the commodity, nor do you pay the full purchase price for the commodity. In reality, you pay about 10 percent of the market price, borrowing the balance from your broker. This practice is known as buying *on margin*. Each futures contract has an expiration date within which you must complete the trade. Therefore, you can't wait out a period of unfavorable prices; you must hope to make a profit soon, or accept your losses.

Trading commodities is highly risky. It's estimated that about 85 percent of all commodities speculators lose money. Part of the reason for this high risk is the many factors that can influence changes in the price of commodities. For example, if bad weather damages crops, commodity shortages and higher prices may result. On the other hand, overproduction or the discovery of new sources of supply can cause prices to fall drastically. It's very hard to predict price changes of this kind.

To minimize the risk involved in commodities trading, many investors are turning to *commodity pools*. A commodity pool is a limited partnership managed by professional commodity traders who pool the funds of many investors to purchase commodity futures contracts. The company forming the pool has the status of *general partner* and controls the operations of the pool. Those who invest in the pool are *limited partners*; that is, possible losses are limited to the amount of money you invest in the pool.

It normally costs $1000 to buy a single unit in a commodity pool. Shares can be redeemed only by selling them back to the pool itself. This can be done by written notice and takes approximately 2 weeks.

Commodity pools have certain advantages similar to those of mutual funds, including diversification, financial strength, professional management, and up-to-date information gleaned from many research sources.

In addition, investment in a commodity pool carries with it an important tax advantage. Even though a commodity futures contract is turned over quickly, the profits are not treated entirely as short-term capital gains. Instead, 60 percent of the profits are normally considered long-term capital gains, and so receive more favorable tax treatment. Commodity trading is the only form of investment to offer this particular tax advantage.

If you're contemplating the purchase of a share in a commodity pool, examine the prospectus carefully. It should inform you about the types of commodities to be traded, how cash distributions will be made, and how withdrawals are handled. The fees should be clearly spelled out. These normally include an up-front load or commission, a start-up fee (averaging 10 percent of your invest-

ment), and other charges, including an account maintenance fee, that may total up to 6 percent of your investment.

To summarize: Both types of investments discussed in
this section—stock options and commodity futures—are
speculative and risky. Both demand specialized expertise
and a strong sense of the likely future direction of prices.
If you understand these points and are willing to accept
the risks involved, you may want to consider adding these
investments to your portfolio.

Treasury Bills, Notes, and Bonds

••

The world's safest investment—obligations of the U.S. government—available in three forms to suit differing investment needs

The U.S. Treasury Department has one of the biggest jobs you can imagine—providing money for the financial needs of the federal government. Much of the money it raises comes from the sale of securities to the general public and institutional investors. These securities—generally known as **Treasury obligations**—can be purchased through commercial banks, brokerage houses, and other financial institutions at a fee. Or they can be purchased without a fee through any of the 12 Federal Reserve Banks in the United States or 1 of their 25 branches.

Treasury obligations are tax-exempt at the state and local levels and are backed by "the full faith and credit" of the United States. The credit risk involved in this form of investment is considered practically nil (despite what you may have heard about 12-digit federal deficits). By comparison with similar obligations issued by corporations, Treasury obligations usually pay a yield which is 1 or 2 percentage points lower. However, many people are willing to accept the slightly lower yield in exchange for almost absolute safety. As the saying goes, you can eat well or sleep well but you can't do both.

Treasury obligations are actively traded in the secondary market, so that they are relatively liquid and not especially vulnerable to price changes. And if you must sell a Treasury obligation, you'll earn interest on it up to the day of sale. Treasury obligations clearly have a number of advantages for the investor.

In this section, you'll learn about three popular types of Treasury obligations: Treasury bills, Treasury notes, and Treasury bonds.

Treasury bills, or *T-bills,* are issued with maturities of 3, 6, and 12 months and sold in minimum amounts of $10,000 and additional multiples of $5000. Like U.S. savings bonds, they are sold at a discount and redeemed, upon maturity, at face value. Thus you receive the interest earned by the T-bill immediately upon purchase, in the form of a discount, rather than during the life of the bill.

T-bills are sold at auction on a regular basis. It is at the auction that the interest rate to be paid is set. It normally results from the competitive bids of large institutional investors. Auctions for 3- and 6-month bills are held every Monday, while auctions for 12-month bills are held every fourth Thursday.

If you buy your T-bill through a bank or broker, you'll be charged a small fee (tax deductible). If you buy your T-bill directly from the Federal Reserve, no fee is charged. Here's how to go about it:

Send or bring your payment for a T-bill in the denomination you prefer to the nearest branch of the Federal Reserve Bank, making sure that it is received prior to 1:00 P.M. eastern standard time on the day of the auction. The payment must be in the form of cash, a certified personal check, a bank check, or matured U.S. Treasury notes or bonds, and it must be for the full face value of the T-bill. When the auction takes place, the interest rate for the bills sold that day is set, and the amount of the discount to which you are entitled is determined accordingly. You are then sent a check for the amount of the discount.

When the maturity date of the T-bill arrives, you can redeem the bill for its full face value. And since you received the interest (in the form of the discount) in advance, the practical yield is actually higher than the nominal interest rate. The following example will show why this is so.

Suppose you buy a $10,000 one-year T-bill with an interest rate set by auction at 9 percent. After paying your $10,000, you'll receive by mail—normally within a week— a check for the 9 percent discount. That comes to $900. Thus the effective price of the T-bill to you is just $9100. Since you've now received $900 income on that $9100 investment, your true yield is 900 divided by 9100, or 9.9 percent—not the nominal 9 percent. And, of course, you're free to take the $900 and invest it somewhere else for the rest of the year, thus increasing your income still further.

For federal income tax purposes, the $900 is considered ordinary income to be reported at the time the T-bill matures, not at the time of purchase. For example, if you buy a 6-month T-bill in July 1986, you'll receive your full discount immediately. However, the amount of the discount is not considered as income until January 1987, when the T-bill matures. Therefore, it would not have to be declared for tax purposes up until April 1988. (Estimated tax is not considered in the example.)

When it's time to redeem your T-bill, if you bought it through a bank or a broker, you'll follow the procedure arranged at the time of purchase. If you bought it directly from a Federal Reserve Bank, you'll automatically receive a check from the Treasury Department. You can automatically roll over—that is, reinvest—your funds in new T-bills by indicating this choice on Form PD4633-2, which the Treasury Department sends to all holders of T-bills.

Treasury notes, like T-bills, pay interest rates determined by auction. However, they are not sold at a discount. Instead, they pay interest every 6 months at a rate fixed at the time of purchase. In this respect, they resemble corporate bonds.

Treasury notes also have a longer life span than T-bills; they mature between 1 and 10 years from the date of issue. Notes that mature in less than 4 years are offered in minimum denominations of $5000, while those maturing in 4 years or longer are sold in minimums of $1000. Treasury note auctions are held on the following schedule: One- and two-year notes are auctioned during the second half of each month. Three-year notes are auctioned during the first week of February, May, August, and November. Four-year notes are auctioned during the second half of March, June, September, and December, and five-year notes are auctioned during February, May, August, and November.

Like corporate bonds, Treasury notes are bought and sold on the secondary market by brokers and banks. The U.S. Treasury doesn't buy back Treasury notes; however, you can exchange notes of one denomination for those of another. The market price for a Treasury note will fluctuate, depending on changes in interest rates; you can find current prices in the financial pages of your newspaper. However, the actual price you'll pay a broker—or the amount you'll receive when selling your notes—will differ from the price shown, due to the broker's fee and the slightly higher costs involved in buying or selling *odd-lot* amounts (which include any purchase of less than $1 million worth of Treasury notes).

When you buy a Treasury note, you can have its ownership registered in any of four ways:

Single Owner: For example, Tom Green (Social Security Number 100-10-1000).

Two Owners: For example, Tom Green (100-10-1000) and Betty Green (200-20-2000).

Joint Tenancy: For example, Tom Green (100-10-1000) or Betty Green (200-20-2000).

Guardian or Custodian for a Minor: For example, Betty Green, guardian (or custodian) for Tom Green, Jr. (300-30-3000).

The note can't be registered solely in the name of a minor. Because Treasury notes are registered, they can be redeemed if lost or stolen by contacting:

Claims and Correspondence Branch
U.S. Treasury Department
Bureau of Public Debt
Washington, DC 20226

Treasury bonds are much like Treasury notes, with a few differences. They have longer maturity periods, ranging from 10 to 30 years. The minimum investment is $1000, with bonds available in denominations of $1000, $5000, $10,000, $100,000, and $1,000,000. Treasury bonds tend to fluctuate in price on the secondary market more than Treasury notes. And some Treasury bonds contain call provisions, allowing the government to redeem the bond at any time within 5 years of the maturity date.

Treasury bonds with 10- and 30-year maturities are auctioned during February, May, August, and November, while 20-year bonds are auctioned during March, June, September, and December. For information on upcoming Treasury auctions or recent interest rates, you can telephone 202-287-4088 twenty-four hours a day.

Humorist Will Rogers once said, "I am not so concerned with the return *on* my investment as I am with the return *of* my investment." If Will had owned Treasury obligations, he wouldn't have needed to worry.

U.S. Savings Bonds

•••

A relatively low-yielding investment that may be right for you if you demand the greatest degree of safety or need to be "forced" into regular saving

If safety is your prime consideration when judging an investment, then U.S. government securities are your best bet. Americans currently own over $67 billion in government securities, and the familiar U.S. savings bond is one of the most popular and convenient of these securities. There are currently two types of U.S. savings bond available—the **Series EE** bond and the **Series HH** bond. In this section, we'll explain both and provide some insight as to their advantages and disadvantages as investment vehicles.

The EE bond is a non-negotiable security against the credit of the U.S. Treasury: *non-negotiable* because once it is purchased it cannot be resold to anyone else but only sold back to the government at a fixed price. The EE bonds are sold at half their face value and are available in denominations of $50, $75, $100, $200, $500, $1000, $5000, and $10,000. Thus you can buy a savings bond for as little as $25, making them a practical choice for the investor with only a minimal amount of money to set aside.

Until fairly recently, U.S. savings bonds paid a notoriously low rate of interest. This has now changed. In 1982, the federal government realized that it was necessary to make savings bonds more competitive with such higher-yielding investments as money market funds. Therefore, the fixed interest schedule formerly used for savings bonds was changed to a variable rate adjusted every 6 months, in May and November. The rate is set at 85 percent of the current average rate on 5-year Treasury securities. There is also a minimum payout of 7½ percent annual interest.

This new variable interest rate is a real boon to investors, since when market interest rates rise, the owner of U.S. savings bonds will now benefit from the higher yields, rather than being locked into a low fixed rate as before. And the 7½ percent minimum rate will protect the investor in case interest rates take a dramatic plunge. For example, if the 5-year Treasury security average rate is 12 percent, your EE bonds will pay 10.2 percent (85 percent of 12 percent). However, if the Treasury rate falls to, say 6 percent, you'll still receive the minimum 7½ percent on your EE bonds. Thus U.S. savings bonds, while still not the highest-paying investment around, now offer a respectable yield along with their unmatched safety. Safety not only for their guarantee of principal and interest but also for their repayment should they be stolen, lost, or destroyed. If any of these situations should occur, bonds can be replaced by notifying:

Bureau of Public Debt
200 Third St.
Parkersburg, WV 26101

Savings bonds are a relatively illiquid investment. You must hold onto your EE bonds for 5 years in order to receive the variable rate (or the 7½ percent minimum, if applicable). If you cash in your bonds before 5 years have passed, they'll earn interest on a fixed, graduated scale which starts at 5½ percent after the first year and increases by ¼ percent for each additional 6 months, up to 5 years. Thereafter, the variable rate applies through the tenth year of the bonds' life, at which time they are mature. This means you are guaranteed that your money will at least double in 10 years, with the possibility of a greater return, depending on interest rates.

The exact timing of your purchase and redemption of savings bonds can make a surprisingly large difference in the amount you'll earn. Here's how it works. First, no matter on what day of the month you buy your EE bond, you'll be credited with interest for the full month. This means that even if you buy the bond on May 31, you'll get credit for interest beginning with May 1.

Later, when you cash in your bond, other rules apply. If you hold the bond for 18 months or less, interest is credited on the first day of each month for the previous month. For example, if you cash in your bond on August 31, you'll receive interest through July 31 only. But if you can wait just 1 more day and cash in the bond on September 1, you'll be credited with interest for the month of August.

If you hold the bond for 19 months or more, interest is credited every 6 months, counting from the month of purchase. For example, if you bought a bond several years ago during August, you would have to wait until February 1 to be sure of receiving interest for the full 6-month August-to-February period. If you cashed in the bond even 1 day too soon, you'd lose 6 months' worth of interest. So take a close look at your calendar before you head to the bank to redeem your bonds. The following rule should be easy to understand: *Whatever month you purchase a bond, make that month the first month of a 6-month cycle and sell the bond in the seventh month.*

When you need information on bond redemption values, you can contact the federal government. Write to:

Office of Public Affairs
U.S. Savings Bond Division
Department of the Treasury
Washington, DC 20266

Ask for Form PD3600.

The interest payout on U.S. savings bonds is tax-exempt on the state and local level; it is tax-deferred on the federal level. That is, the interest you receive is paid in one lump sum at the time of redemption and is fully taxable in that year. You can avoid a heavy tax liability by buying savings bonds in your child's name and treating each year's interest income as reportable as earned. Here's how it works: File a tax return for your youngster in the year you buy the bond. This shows the IRS that you intend to report the interest income from the bond *annually*, rather than all upon redemption. Since your child probably has a small annual income, the interest earned will be, in effect, tax-free. But note that once the child elects to declare the EE income annually, he or she must do so with all future bonds purchased.

If you intend to use this method to save on taxes, be sure to take two precautions: First, save a copy of your child's income tax form until after you've redeemed the bonds. Second, don't put your name, or anyone else's, on the bond as co-owner. The instrument must be in the child's name only, so that the child is presumed to be the owner, no matter who paid for the bond. Thus this tax-saving technique is most appropriate for use with bonds that are intended for savings to benefit the child—a college tuition fund, for example.

U.S. savings bonds are easy to buy. They're available for purchase at any bank or post office. You can also buy them on a regular basis through your employer's payroll-deduction plan. This is a very valuable service for those who find it hard to save unless forced to do so. With payroll deduction, the money to buy your bonds is taken out of your salary check before you see it, thus reducing the pain involved in saving and eliminating the temptation to spend the money rather than put it aside. Examine your saving history honestly. If you've had trouble sticking to a saving plan, consider the advantages of investing in savings bonds through a payroll-deduction plan.

Up to this point, we've been discussing EE bonds only. The HH bonds are different in several ways. Unlike EE bonds, HH bonds pay interest on a semiannual basis. Therefore, the interest income is taxable as it is earned throughout the life of the bond. The HH bonds mature in 10 years, pay 7½ percent interest annually, and are available in denominations of $500, $1000, $5000, and $10,000.

You can't buy HH bonds for cash, however. They are available only by exchanging EE bonds (or the older E bonds) for HH bonds. There is no limit on the amount of the exchange; your EEs must be at least 6 months old before they can be exchanged. The exchange can be made at any Federal Reserve Bank, but most banks selling EE bonds can provide Form PD3253, which is used in arranging the exchange. Any month after June is a good time to make the switch. For example, by swapping EE bonds for HH bonds during July 1986 the first payment of HH interest to you won't be made until January 1987. This means that you will not have to declare that income until 1988 when you file your 1987 return.

Why would anyone turn in their EE bonds to get HH bonds? It's a way of stretching out and so limiting the income tax liability that goes along with the lump-sum interest payout characteristic of EE bonds. The interest payable on your mature EE bonds isn't taxable at the time you exchange them for HH bonds. Instead, the amount of interest accumulated on the EE bonds is stamped on the face of the HH bonds. That amount is not taxable as current income until you cash in your HH bonds, which may not happen for quite a while—not until after retirement, for example, at which time your income and tax bracket will be lower. If you're planning on retiring fairly soon, it's a good idea to exchange your EE bonds for HH bonds, rather than simply cashing them in. That way, you'll end up having to return less of the profits to Uncle Sam.

Zero Coupon Bonds

••

The ideal investment for those who consider "outcome" more important than "income": a bond that pays a big return all at once, at redemption time

The *zero coupon bond* is a unique financial tool which is increasingly popular as a long-term investment. As you'll see, zero coupon bonds have certain advantages which make them excellent choices for your individual retirement account or for your child's college savings plan.

Like any bond, a zero coupon bond is a debt obligation issued by a corporation or by an agency of the federal, state, or local government. When you buy a bond, you are buying a promise from the issuing institution to pay the amount on the face of the bond at the date of maturity. In these respects, a zero coupon bond is like any other bond.

However, unlike traditional bonds, "zeros" are sold at a price well below the face value. The discount is usually from 65 to 75 percent. For example, a zero with a face value of $1000 may sell for just $311. You pay $311 today; at the time of maturity—usually in 10 years—you can redeem the bond for its full $1000 face value. The extra $689 paid on redemption is the accumulated 10 years' worth of interest on your $311 investment.

Table 4.   Zero Coupon Bonds

Interest Rate	MATURITY DATE		
	10 Years	20 Years	30 Years
8%	$456	$208	$95
10%	$377	$142	$54
12%	$311	$ 97	$30

During the life of the zero, you clip no coupons and receive no interest payments. (Hence the name "zero coupon bonds.") The entire interest payout comes at once—upon redemption.

Table 4 shows the price you'd have to pay for a $1000 zero coupon bond based on various interest rates and maturity dates. (The amounts are rounded to the nearest dollar.) Naturally, the longer the term of the bond and the higher the interest rate, the greater the discount at which the bond is sold. If you're still in your twenties or thirties, you can buy a big chunk of retirement money very cheaply by buying a long-term zero right now. For example, at a 10 percent interest rate, you can buy a zero redeemable at $1000 in 30 years for only $54! It's hard to imagine a better buy than that.

Zero coupon bonds offer several distinct advantages. Zeros have *call protection,* meaning that it is unlikely that they will be called in for early redemption by the issuing company. (There'd be no advantage to the corporation in prepaying the interest on zeros.) Zeros also offer liquidity. If, for some reason, you need to sell your bond before maturity, you can sell it on the so-called secondary market at the prevailing rate.

Most important, zeros adapt themselves very well to a

variety of personal financial plans. Because you know exactly how much money you'll be receiving for your investment and exactly when the payout will occur, you can make long-range plans based on your investment in zeros. Thus, they make an excellent choice for your individual retirement account or Keogh plan investment, allowing you to accumulate tax-deferred interest at a fixed rate until retirement.

They are also an excellent way of saving for your child's college tuition needs. By establishing a custodial account for your child under the Uniform Gift to Minors Act (UGMA), you can invest in zeros which will mature at the time your child is ready for school and, at the same time, greatly reduce or minimize the tax bite on the interest. Since the interest income will be credited to your child's account, taxes will be paid at his or her low tax bracket rate. Your accountant or broker can tell you how to set up an appropriate custodial account.

However, zero coupon bonds do have some disadvantages. The degree of risk is one. If the company issuing the bonds is no longer solvent at the time of maturity, you may lose your entire investment. The possibility of default is a serious consideration with bonds of every kind, but the problem is especially significant with zeros. This is because you receive all interest payments at once, upon maturity, whereas with other types of bonds you receive interest on a regular basis throughout the life of the bond.

A second disadvantage involves the markup that brokers add to the wholesale price of the bonds. It is very difficult for an investor to determine what the markup is on zero coupon bonds because the bonds are sold "net." The only way to know whether your broker is charging you a fair price is to shop around. Call up other brokerage houses to see what the competition has to offer. Remember that the larger the broker's markup, the more the bond will cost, leaving you with a smaller "yield."

A third disadvantage involves taxes. Although you receive no cash payments during the life of the zero coupon bond, you are taxed as if you do. For example, suppose you purchase a zero coupon bond with a face value of $1000 due in 10 years for a discounted price of $400. The $600 interest is treated for tax purposes as if you were being paid $60 worth of interest during each of the bond's 10 years of life. The taxation on this "invisible interest" can be considered a drawback of zero coupon bonds. Remember, however, that if your bonds are being bought as part of a saving plan for your children, you can minimize or eliminate the tax bite by setting up a custodial account as described above.

Furthermore, there is another option for those who wish to avoid paying taxes on the income from a zero coupon bond. This is the *zero coupon municipal bond.* As the name implies, this is a bond which performs the same as a corporate zero coupon bond but is issued by a state or local government agency. Because it is a municipal bond, the interest you earn is exempt from all federal taxes and, in many cases, from state and local taxes as well. The gains you receive at maturity are considered tax-free income which has accrued annually from the time of the issuance of the bonds and which need not be declared on your tax return.

Those attracted to zero coupon bonds should also consider one more alternative: zeros issued by the U.S. Treasury. These are sometimes called by other names, such as *stripped Treasuries,* a name given by brokerage houses which "strip" smaller investment units from large Treasury bonds for sale to investors. Zero coupon Treasury bonds are sold in units of varying sizes; many different maturity dates, with varying interest rates, are offered. Tell your broker when you'd like your bonds to mature, and he or she can let you know when zeros that meet your needs are available. Naturally, zero coupon Treasury bonds are an exceptionally safe investment—like other U.S. government securities.

The most valuable feature of the zero coupon bond is that it lets you know exactly how much money you'll have at a particular future date. This facilitates financial planning. In addition, buying zeros allows you to lock in interest rates for a long investment period—an important consideration if you feel that the long-term trend of interest rates is downward. All in all, zero coupon bonds are an investment that's well worth investigating.

PART TWO

....

Knowing Your Estate

Divorce and Taxes

•••

Divorce doesn't necessarily involve only a husband and a wife. The big winner in the settlement is often a third party—the Internal Revenue Service.

Getting a divorce is never pleasant. It's obviously an emotionally wrenching and difficult experience. Unfortunately, the financial ramifications of getting a divorce only add to the difficulty of the situations. If you're considering a divorce or are in the process of becoming divorced, you should understand some of the problems you'll have to address.

Divorce has always presented certain complicated income tax questions for both parties. The treatment of some of these issues has recently changed as a result of the Tax Reform Act of 1984. Let's take a look at these changes and the income tax situation they create for a divorced couple.

The three divorce-related areas most directly affected by the 1984 law are alimony and child support payments, property transfers between spouses, and exemptions for dependent children.

Alimony and Child Support Payments: Under the new law, as under the old, alimony payments from husband to wife are deductible from the husband's income and taxable as part of the wife's income. (Note: Throughout this discussion, we'll speak as if all alimony and child support payments are made by husbands to wives, since this is the most common situation.) Child support payments, as before, are not deductible by the husband, nor are they taxable for the wife. However, under the old law, any payments not specifically designated as child support payments were considered alimony. This has now changed. Any payment from husband to wife which is intended for the benefit of the child no longer qualifies as alimony.

Here's an example. Suppose a divorce settlement includes an agreement that alimony payments will drop by $150 per month in the event that a dependent child dies, marries, or otherwise ceases to be dependent. Under the new law, $150 of the monthly alimony check would be classified not as alimony but as child support. Since child support payments are nondeductible for the husband, the new law acts as a disincentive for divorced men to give large payments on behalf of their children to their former wives. A greater burden on divorced wives is likely to result.

There are other tax rules pertaining to alimony which you should know. To qualify for tax-deductible status, alimony payments of more than $10,000 per year must be required by the terms of the divorce settlement for at least 6 years and the amount of the payments may not vary by more than $10,000 per year. The purpose of the rule is to enforce the taxable status of lump-sum property settlements. If either qualification is not met—if alimony payments cease prior to the end of the 6-year period or if they vary by some amount greater than $10,000—the Internal Revenue Service (IRS) is entitled to go back through the husband's past returns and tax the amounts which were formerly deducted as alimony.

Two more changes in the law are of note. Husbands deducting alimony payments must now furnish the social security number of the ex-wife to whom the payments are made. (This allows the IRS to trace divorced women who fail to report alimony payments as income.) And women receiving alimony payments may consider them income for the purpose of determining how much money they are eligible to place in an individual retirement account.

Property Transfers: Under the 1984 tax law, the transfer of property from one spouse to another is a nontaxable transaction. The spouse receiving the property must assume the original tax cost of the property. If it is sold at some future date for any price greater than its original cost, the capital gain which results is taxable to the spouse selling the property. (The old law made the capital gain taxable to the spouse who transferred the property, with the tax payable at the time of the transfer. In effect, the transfer between spouses was treated as a sale, even though no money changed hands.)

The new law makes it advantageous from a tax point of view for a spouse to transfer property with a low original cost and a high current value to his or her spouse at the time of divorce. The law covers not only such property items as houses but also financial instruments, such as annuities, life insurance policies, and trusts.

Exemptions for Dependent Children: Rules concerning the tax exemption on children of divorced parents have changed. Under the new law, the spouse who has custody of the child is entitled to claim the income tax exemption for that child, regardless of any child support payments that may be made. It might be possible for a husband, for example, to provide child support payments to his ex-wife which paid for 100 percent of the child's living expenses. In that situation, the wife would still be entitled to claim the exemption. However, a spouse can waive the right to claim an exemption by written agreement between the two parties.

The new law, however, allows either or both of the parents to claim a medical deduction for any health-care costs incurred on behalf their child. Formerly, only the parent claiming the exemption for that child could claim the medical expense deduction.

As you can see, the Tax Reform Act of 1984 effected some important changes in the tax status of divorced individuals. Make sure that you understand their implications if you find yourself planning a divorce settlement.

Early Retirement

••

Before they hand you the gold watch, make sure you're financially ready to enjoy the good life you've been dreaming about.

Many Americans cherish no fonder wish than the hope of retiring early to a comfortable life of leisure, travel, hobbies, and relaxation. If you're lucky—and if you've planned your financial future wisely—this dream will come true for you. But before you opt for early retirement, take a good look at the economic implications of the decision. In this section, we'll explain some of the facts you should know.

For most people, Social Security is a significant part of their retirement income plan. If you retire at age 65, you'll receive your full Social Security benefit, sometimes called your ***primary insurance amount*** (***PIA***). If you retire 3 years early, at age 62, you'll receive only 80 percent of your PIA. For each additional month you work after reaching age 62, the amount of your monthly Social Security payments will increase by 5/9 of 1 percent of the benefit at age 62.

An example will show you how significant this difference can become. Using 1985 figures, the approximate annual Social Security benefit for someone at the maximum employee contribution level would be $6980 if he or she retired at age 62. By age 65, the annual benefit would increase to $8730, and by age 70, to $10,120.

Because of cost-of-living adjustments and other changes, these figures will probably be slightly different by the time you retire, but the point they illustrate remains the same. You must carefully weigh the value of early retirement against the financial loss you'll probably incur.

Of course, how long you live after retirement—which no one can predict with certainty—will help determine which retirement age is most financially beneficial for you. For example, using the figures above, you would have to collect the higher age-65 benefit for approximately 12 years to make up for the 3 years' worth of smaller benefits received by the early retiree between ages 62 and 65. Will you live to collect benefits for those 12 years? Will you, perhaps, live many years longer? Who can say? The ultimate decision as to when you should retire remains a very personal one, in which financial considerations are only one factor.

People often ask whether it makes any difference what time of the year you retire as far as Social Security benefits are concerned. In general, the answer is no. Most people in fact retire toward the end of a calendar year simply as a matter of convenience and personal preference. However, the Social Security law permits you to retire at any time during the year without forfeiting any benefits; payments start any month you choose, provided you meet all the conditions of eligibility.

When you've set your retirement date, plan on applying for Social Security benefits about 3 months early. This leaves plenty of time to process your claim and handle any questions or problems that may arise.

Even more important, plan on making good use of

your newfound freedom after retirement. In this country, we've put more effort into helping people reach old age than into helping them enjoy it. Be prepared, because you will find yourself with literally thousands of hours to fill each year—hours that can be spent on creative, spiritually nourishing, life-enhancing activities or on growing bored, tired, and old. It's important to be financially ready for retirement, but being psychologically and emotionally ready is harder and even more important. During the years between now and your retirement—whenever it comes—you should be preparing in all these ways.

Federal Deposit Insurance

••

How safe is the money you deposit in a bank or savings and loan?
Here are the reassuring facts.

Bank failures, which many Americans came to regard as
vestiges of the 1930s, have been in the news again recently.
In the unsettled economic climate of the late 1970s and
early 1980s, some banks, including a few large ones, tot-
tered on the verge of bankruptcy, and some fell in. What
are the implications of this for small savers, who may have
most or all of their money deposited in banks? Is there any
cause of alarm?

The short answer is almost certainly no. Since the
Great Depression, an extensive federally supported system of insurance corporations has been established to
guarantee the safety of deposits in banks and savings and
loan institutions. Today, virtually all savings institutions
are insured by one of these corporations.

For example, of the over 15,000 commercial and mutual savings banks in the United States, all but about 600
are insured by the Federal Deposit Insurance Corporation
(FDIC). Of the nearly 3500 savings and loan associations,
nearly 3000 are insured by the Federal Savings and Loan

Insurance Corporation (FSLIC). The others are covered by state or private insurance plans.

As you can see, the chances are that almost any bank or savings and loan you might consider depositing your money in is covered by insurance. You can tell which agency insures your bank by looking for the seal of membership displayed at bank entrances and tellers' windows.

The types of financial instruments covered by insurance up to $100,000 include:

Savings accounts

Checking accounts

Holiday or vacation club accounts

Letters of credit

Money market accounts

Certificates of deposit (CDs)

Uninvested trust funds

Certified checks

Cashier's checks

Money orders

If you owned a CD of $75,000 and had a money market account of $40,000 at the same bank, you would be insured up to a maximum of $100,000 for both accounts, even though they total $115,000. This maximum does not take into account any amounts deposited in another insured bank. When a bank has several branches, the main office and all branch offices are considered one bank. Individual retirement account (IRA) and Keogh plan funds held in trust or in a custodial capacity by a bank are insured separately from any other deposits owned by the same investor—each to a maximum of $100,000. If you have both an individual account and a joint account at the same bank, each account is insured separately to the $100,000 maximum.

What would happen in the unlikely event of a bank failure? First, government bank regulators would step in and liquidate all the assets of the bank. To the money obtained in this way would be added sufficient additional funds from the insurance corporation to allow for the repayment of all insured funds. Within 2 weeks, each depositor would receive a check for the full amount of his or her insured account.

Deposits exceeding the insurable limits are not guaranteed. If you have uninsured funds deposited in a bank which fails, it's likely that you'll ultimately receive only a percentage of your money back, after waiting on line with the bank's other creditors for your share of the liquidated assets.

If you have any questions about the insurance on your bank deposits, you can telephone the FDIC's toll-free number, 800-424-4334.

Financial Planning
for Women

●●

No matter what your age or marital status, you owe it to yourself to develop a financial plan to protect your future independently.

Here's a statistic that may surprise you: Out of all females over the age of 21, approximately 85 percent will die as single women. How is this possible? Out of every 100 women, 6 never marry. Of the remaining 94, 33 have marriages that end in divorce and 46 outlive their husbands. The implication is simple: The chances are excellent that at some time in a woman's life, she will be alone and forced to manage her own finances. If you're presently single, you already understand this. If you're married, please read on.

The first point is the most essential. As a married woman, you should consider yourself *financially separate* from your husband. This is so even though he may supply most of your family's income and handle many or most of the financial decisions. You should make a financial plan of your own and provide for the likelihood that eventually you'll be managing your money independently.

A good place to start is by opening personal checking and savings accounts and obtaining one or more credit cards in your name only. Why is this necessary? Because a woman whose assets are entirely tied up in joint accounts with her husband, and whose credit cards are all in her husband's name, may face severe financial problems in the future. If you become divorced or widowed, your credit history will be based entirely on your husband's finances, not your own. You may learn, to your dismay, that you lack the financial standing to qualify for your own line of credit. When financial need strikes, this can be a devastating handicap. Remember that money never changes, only pockets.

Furthermore, any money held in a joint account with your husband may be frozen by the bank or financial institution upon his death, leaving you with no access to funds until after your husband's estate is settled. And in the event of divorce, you may find all jointly held funds divided equally, even though you may have contributed more to some accounts. There are other reasons for establishing your own savings, checking, and credit accounts.

Next, you should begin to develop an independent retirement plan, one not based on assumptions about your husband's contributions. This may be an uphill struggle. The U.S. retirement system depends largely on Social Security and private pension plans, both of which are directly tied to the number of years an individual has spent in the work force. However, the career patterns of women differ greatly from those of men, largely because of the time most women devote to raising their children but also because of other factors, such as the willingness of most women to relocate—and sacrifice their own seniority as employees—when their husbands' careers demand it.

As a result of these "liabilities," working women often fail to remain on the job long enough to qualify for their own pension plan. In fact, fewer than 20 percent of women over the age of 62 ever receive their own pensions.

Nor is it safe to count on your husband's pension for your own retirement. Not only is there the possibility of a marital breakup, but some private pension plans will not protect you in the event of your husband's death. For example, many pension plans offer an optional *joint-and-survivor* clause, which allows pension payments to continue after the retired spouse dies. If your husband waives this option in order to receive higher benefits up front, you'll lose the pension income when your husband dies. (And until recently, employees could waive this option without informing their spouses. Fortunately, federal legislation has been changed to forbid this.) Let me explain:

The law now mandates that formal consent of a spouse (usually the wife) must be given if the employee (usually the husband) wants to waive a provision which provides his wife with retirement benefits after his demise. The purpose of this law is designed to provide some retirement income for widowed women. For example, a married employee must take an option for retirement benefits in a form which will provide his spouse with some pension income after his death. The one exception to this law is the written consent (notarized) on the part of the spouse to waive this most needed protection. The new law materialized because of abuses in the pension system. Many male workers had dropped any protection for their spouses (known as joint-and-survivor benefits) without informing their wives. The reason for their action resulted from the joint-and-survivor benefit clause. If this clause were part of the contract (in other words, protecting the wife), the pension payments to the husband upon his retirement would be smaller. If this protection for the wife was dropped, the worker would then increase his monthly pension income. However it also would stop payments to his family upon his death. Now the law protects the spouse.

Another provision now protects survivors of employees who die before they reach the early retirement age of 55. The new requirement, which can be waived if both the worker and spouse reject this benefit in writing, now states that preretirement death benefits must be paid to the spouse of any married employee who has earned vested rights in the business pension plan. When accepted, the surviving spouse will receive a guaranteed monthly income for life beginning in the year the deceased worker would have been 55 years old. This is advantageous for older workers but does little for young people who have not worked long enough to accumulate any meaningful benefits. For example, suppose that a 30-year-old male employee, who has earned the right to a pension of $400 per month at retirement, dies before reaching 31. His widow may receive only $75 per month (approximate), 25 years from the date of his death when her husband would have been 55. This small amount (based upon reductions for the joint-and-survivor option and for taking benefits before the normal retirement age of 65) certainly would not be meaningful for the widow and her family. What should you do in this case? Because most companies pass on the charge for this protection to the employee (by reducing the amount of pension that he and his spouse would receive upon his retirement), it may make more sense to waive this option and buy life insurance which would supply to the family immediate cash upon his death. In this way, the family would not have to accept a permanent pension reduction which is never used because the employee lived past age 55 or, if he should die before, will not be paid to his wife until he would have reached 55. Therefore, a young couple should waive their right of benefit and buy life insurance for their protection. Under the present ruling, a couple can always change their mind and opt to take the coverage in their later years when the husband nears retirement age or if his health should decline.

The point, then, is that married women, whether working outside the home or not, must plan for retirement independently of their husbands. You should develop your own savings and investment plan with a definite goal to be attained by retirement age. You should open your own individual retirement account, invested in financial instruments appropriate for your age and income. And you should become as fully informed about your family's finances as your husband.

One more point: Every woman should have her own will and keep it up to date. It could even be argued that a wife's will is more essential than her husband's, since, in most cases, she will outlive him and thus be responsible for not one but two estates—his and hers. This is so even when a wife has few assets of her own. Consider this scenario: A husband dies, leaving all his property to his wife. Shortly afterward, she dies *intestate*—that is, without a will. All the family's assets would be disposed of according to the laws of intestacy applicable in her state. The results may or may not be in accordance with her wishes.

Of course, we've only touched on a few of the important financial topics on which a wife should inform herself. In a sense, if you're a married woman, you should consider everything else in this book as an extension of this discussion. The point is: You owe it to yourself to learn as much about personal finances as possible, so that when the time comes for all the family financial decisions to fall into your lap, rather than your husband's, you'll be prepared.

Joint Ownership

●●

There are three different forms of joint ownership, each with its distinctive features. It's important to understand the differences.

Joint ownership is the most common method by which married couples take title to their house and other assets. It may also be used by others who wish to share the control of some property. Let's examine the three basic types of joint ownership, each of which has certain special legal and financial characteristics you should know about. They are called ***joint tenancy, tenancy in common,*** and ***community property.***

Joint Tenancy: With this method of ownership, both owners have a complete and undivided interest in the property. Neither owner can sell or transfer his or her interest in the property without the consent of the other. When one owner dies, the property immediately passes to the surviving owner without having to go to ***probate*** (the acceptance of the will of the deceased by an appropriate court). For joint tenancy to be in effect, the names of both owners must appear on the deed or other ownership document.

Both married couples and single people used joint tenancy as a method of guaranteeing ease of transfer of property upon the death of one of the owners. However, it can't be considered a substitute for a will since joint tenancy may not automatically produce the desired results after death. For example, suppose you and your sister buy a summer home together, taking title as joint tenants. You die first, and your sister dies shortly thereafter. Upon your death, your share in the summer home reverts immediately to your sister. Therefore, when she dies, the home goes entirely to her heirs; your own heirs will receive no share in it. This may or may not be what you intended.

Tenancy in Common: Under this method, each owner has title to half the property. If one owner dies, his or her share does not automatically pass to the survivor. Instead, it is disposed of in accordance with the will of the deceased. This method is used by friends or relatives who wish to form a joint ownership and share in its benefits while they are alive but want to retain the right to decide individually what happens to their share of the property when they die.

Community Property: In certain states, husband and wife share equally in any property either one accumulates while they are living together. This is so regardless of whose name appears on the deed or ownership papers. Such jointly owned property is called *community property,* and the states where this is a matter of law are called "community property states." At the present time, the following states are community property states:

Arizona	New Mexico
California	Nevada
Idaho	Texas
Louisiana	Washington

There are exceptions to the community property law: (1) property obtained by either spouse prior to the marriage, (2) property acquired after marriage by gift or inheritance, and (3) property acquired in non-community property states.

Note that the fact that you have moved from a community property state to a non-community property state does not automatically exempt you from the community property law. You are still subject to the law for property you obtained while a resident of the community property state.

Lump-Sum
Distributions

•••

*Some tips on ways to avoid a big tax bite on your lump-sum pension
distribution*

Every day, for various reasons, people are receiving large
lump-sum distributions representing the accumulated values of their pension plans. This may occur when you retire, or it may occur sooner if you become disabled, if you
leave your present employer, or if the company decides to
terminate your pension plan. In any case, when you receive such a lump-sum distribution, you face a problem:
How do you minimize the taxes on this, often sizable, payment?

There are basically two solutions: (1) 10-year forward
averaging for tax purposes and (2) an individual retirement account (IRA) rollover. We'll consider both these
techniques.

Ten-Year Forward Averaging: You may be acquainted
with ordinary income averaging, which is a way of reducing your income taxes for a year in which your income is
markedly higher than in previous years. Ten-year forward
averaging is slightly different in that it allows your lump-

sum distribution to be taxed at a different, lower rate than your other income. Here's how it works.

When you use 10-year forward averaging, your lump-sum distribution is taxed as if you were receiving it in 10 equal annual payments. For each of the 10 years, you pay taxes on just one-tenth of the total distribution. Furthermore, the tax on each installment is computed as though the lump-sum distribution was your only source of income for the year. This amount is then added to your other income tax payments for the year. The tax is likely to be far less than it would be if computed as part of your entire year's income. In fact, many people can reduce the taxes they pay on their lump-sum distribution by as much as two-thirds using the 10-year forward averaging method.

Compute the amount of your tax under the 10-year forward averaging plan using IRS Form 4972. Your accountant or tax adviser can provide you with additional information on this useful money-saving method.

IRA Rollover: Another way to reduce the taxes on your lump-sum distribution is to roll it over—that is, reinvest it—in an IRA. This must be done within 60 days of receiving the distribution; otherwise, you lose the tax-shelter status otherwise conferred by the IRA. You don't have to pay any current income taxes on the distribution amount if you deposit it in an IRA, nor will you owe taxes on the income which accumulates in the account. The IRA funds become taxable only upon withdrawal, which may begin after you reach age 59½ and must begin by age 70½.

Which method—10-year averaging or IRA rollover— is better for you? The answer depends on your personal financial situation. If you plan to retire and liquidate your IRA in a short time—say, 4 years or less—then the 10-year forward averaging method is likely to save you more money. This is because, once you begin withdrawing your IRA funds, the money is usually taxed at a higher rate than that called for under 10-year averaging.

Another consideration is the level of income you expect to enjoy after retirement. If you expect your income to decline sharply upon retirement, then an IRA rollover plan is probably your best choice. Chances are that, under those circumstances, the taxes you'll pay when withdrawing your IRA funds will be relatively low. On the other hand, if income from other sources will keep you in a fairly high tax bracket when you retire, then the 10-year forward averaging plan is best. Pay the low 10-year averaging tax rate and invest the distribution amount in an appropriate tax-saving instrument, such as municipal bonds. As with most financial decisions, several factors must be taken into account, and only you can decide which is most important to you.

The Safe-Deposit Box

••

Even if you already rent a safe-deposit box, you probably don't know the laws governing access to them—but you should.

Most people have access to a **safe-deposit box** at a local bank. They're quite inexpensive to rent, and they make a convenient, safe place for storage of valuable items, such as jewelry, bonds, and difficult-to-replace papers. However, you should understand the basic rules that apply to safe-deposit boxes. Otherwise, you or your loved ones may find themselves facing an awkward and inconvenient situation when you die. Here's why.

A safe-deposit box may be leased by an individual lessee or by two co-lessees. If the lessee of a box dies, the box may be sealed immediately so that it may be determined whether any taxes are owed on the contents of the box. This involves an inventory conducted by a state tax agent in the presence of a bank official and a representative of the deceased person's estate. Of course, if you live in a large city, the likelihood of the bank's finding out about the death of a lessee is slim; therefore, it's not probable that the box will be sealed. On the other hand, in a small

182

town, a death is usually common knowledge very quickly, and the box will probably be sealed.

If you're involved in a situation with a sealed box, several steps should be taken. The executor of the deceased person's estate should obtain a letter of administration from the appropriate state court in order to examine the contents of the box. If the box contains a will, the court will grant a will search order, requiring the bank to deliver the will to the court. If you're the executor of the estate, make certain that you get such an order, even if a will exists elsewhere, since a more recent will may be contained in the box.

The executor is not personally responsible for the safety or proper disposal of the contents of the box until authorization to obtain the box's contents is granted by the court. When that authorization is given, the executor becomes responsible for distributing the assets contained in the box according to the wishes of the deceased.

As you can see, getting into a safe-deposit box after the death of its lessee isn't always easy. Therefore, certain items should not be kept in a safe-deposit box. These include cash, deeds for cemetery plots, and the only copy of a will. And, of course, any personal or confidential items which you wouldn't want revealed after your death should be kept elsewhere.

Finally, don't assume that one co-lessee is entitled to the contents of a safe-deposit box after the death of the other. Think of two roommates sharing an apartment. If one of them dies, the other is entitled to inherit only the property left to him or her in the will. The co-lessee of a safe-deposit box is in the same position as a roommate and has no more legal right to the contents of the box than anyone else.

Taxation of Social Security

··

Current law makes Social Security benefits partially taxable for some individuals. Determining how you're affected—and what you can do about it—can be complicated.

The Tax Reform Act of 1984 introduced many changes in the computation of individual income taxes. Among the changes were some which affect retired people. Unfortunately, the changes are both complex and, in some ways, unfair. In this section, we'll review the current law and suggest some effective ways of dealing with its implications for you.

Under the provisions of the 1984 law, a formula is used to determine the degree to which Social Security benefits are subject to income tax. This formula sets a "threshold income" below which benefits are not taxed. The threshold is $25,000 for single individuals, $32,000 for a married couple filing a joint return. Those whose income exceeds the threshold amount may be subject to income tax on up to one-half of their Social Security benefits.

To determine whether you exceed the threshold, you must first compute what's called your *modified adjusted gross income*. This consists of your adjusted gross income plus any otherwise tax-free interest income. For example, income derived from tax-free municipal bonds must be included in this calculation. To this sum, add one-half of your Social Security benefits. Then compare this total with the threshold figure. If it exceeds the threshold, your Social Security benefits are partially subject to taxation. The amount of taxable benefits is either half the amount by which you exceed the threshold or half of your Social Security benefits, whichever is less.

If you're confused, don't worry. The following example may clarify the computation. Mr. and Mrs. Brown file a joint tax return. They have an adjusted gross income of $26,000, interest income which is exempt from federal income tax in the amount of $6000, and Social Security benefits of $8000. Here's how they figure their taxable benefits:

$26,000	Adjusted gross income
+ 6,000	Tax-free interest income
32,000	Modified adjusted gross income
+ 4,000	Half of Social Security benefits
$36,000	

Now, the Browns compare this $36,000 figure with their threshold figure. For a married couple filing jointly, the threshold is $32,000. The Browns exceed this by $4000. Therefore, their Social Security benefits are taxable in the amount of either half the excess or half their total benefits. Half the excess is $2000; this is smaller than half of the Browns' Social Security benefits, so $2000 is the amount of their benefits that is taxable.

For comparison's sake, let's change the example slightly. Suppose the Browns' tax-free interest income was $16,000, rather than $6000. Their computation would now be as follows:

$26,000 Adjusted gross income
+16,000 Tax-free interest income
42,000 Modified adjusted gross income
+ 4,000 Half of Social Security benefits
$46,000

This amount exceeds the threshold by $14,000. Half the excess is $7000; half of the Browns' Social Security benefits is $4000. Since the latter figure is the smaller of the two, $4000 is the amount of the Browns' taxable benefits.

As you can see, this relatively new law adversely affects retirees with a high income, whether from tax-free or taxable sources. Those in the 50 percent tax bracket could lose up to one-quarter of their total Social Security benefits in taxes.

An important additional point: The threshold for married couples filing jointly is $32,000, as noted above. However, the threshold for married couples filing *separately* is zero. This has been set in order to prevent married couples from escaping all taxation of Social Security benefits by filing separately, shifting all taxable income to one partner and all Social Security benefits to the other. Therefore, no matter what you may have heard, you will *not* benefit by filing separate returns, rather than a single joint return.

What can you do to minimize the adverse effect of this law? Here are some suggestions.

If you're presently nearing retirement and have to choose whether to receive a lump-sum pension distribution this year or regular annuity payments in future years, take the lump-sum payment right now. The reason is simple. The lump-sum payment will not be subject to the Social Security benefits calculation this year, since you haven't retired yet. And it *will* qualify for a lower tax rate under the 10-year forward averaging plan. By contrast, if you choose the annuity payout plan, you may find that the payments after retirement will push your income to the threshold level, thereby making your retirement benefits subject to tax.

Another tax-saving tactic is to make a gift of tax-free investment instruments to your children. Municipal bonds are an example of instruments that can be used for this purpose. Your children, in turn, can return the interest payments to you in the form of a gift, which is not included in the Social Security computation. Of course, your children will then own the bonds. You must decide whether this is a reasonable option for yourself.

Trusts

Not just for the wealthy, a trust can help you save on taxes while making sure that your money goes to benefit those you most want to help.

A trust involves the transfer of money or other assets from one person, known as the **grantor,** to another, known as the **trustee,** to be managed and used for the benefit of a third person, known as the **beneficiary.** If you establish a trust, you are the grantor; the trustee may be some other individual, an institution, such as a bank or brokerage firm, or, in some cases, yourself.

Establishing a trust can be beneficial in several ways. It can help you reduce your income tax and estate tax liability and can provide a vehicle by which your assets can quickly go to work for your heirs after your death. However, setting up a trust requires the help of a lawyer experienced in estate and tax planning. You'll find that, although the fees charged by such lawyers are high, the advice they offer is essential.

There are two basic types of trusts: the **testamentary trust** and the **living trust.**

The testamentary trust is designed to take effect after the death of the grantor. It is usually established in order to provide an income for the beneficiary while limiting, to some extent, the ways in which the assets may be managed. Property bequeathed through a testamentary trust is part of the estate of the grantor; therefore, the trust takes effect only after the will is probated (that is, accepted by an appropriate state court), which can be a lengthy and costly process.

The assets in the trust are not subject to federal estate taxes so long as their value remains below a legal maximum. (The maximum exempted amount, as of 1986, was $500,000; it is scheduled to increase to $600,000 in 1987.) In addition, property left in trust to a spouse may qualify for an unlimited tax exemption as a *qualified terminable interest property* (*QTIP*) trust. A QTIP trust must contain income-producing property held on condition that the spouse receive the income for life. Upon his or her death, the assets are distributed according to prespecified conditions.

The living trust takes effect during the grantor's lifetime. There are two main kinds of living trusts: *revocable trusts* and *irrevocable trusts*. A revocable trust allows the grantor to change any provisions in the trust at any time, and all income from the trust is taxable to the grantor. With an irrevocable trust, the provisions established by the grantor may not be altered later. The grantor gives up all rights to the assets in the irrevocable trust, and income from the trust is taxable to the beneficiary. (Since the beneficiary is often a child, it is desirable to have the assets taxed at the beneficiary's lower rate.)

Establishing a living trust can be an effective tax-saving strategy, especially useful for those wishing to save for their children's education. Two methods of meeting this goal are described below—the *Clifford trust* and the *Crown loan*.

The Clifford Trust: This is a form of trust designed for parents who want to build up an educational fund for their children but wish to get back the invested principal in the end. It involves shifting the ownership of assets from your tax bracket to your child's lower one. The interest earned by the property belongs to the child, who pays taxes on it at his or her low tax rate. After 10 years and 1 day, the principal is returned to the parent, while the child keeps the interest.

A Clifford trust is a good choice for the investor who is able to set aside a sizable amount of money or other assets for 10 years without touching them. The trust must be large enough to produce sufficient income to make the arrangement worthwhile. Consult a lawyer to make sure that your arrangements qualify for Clifford trust status. If they don't, you as the grantor may be forced to pay taxes on all income produced by the trust.

The Crown Loan: This is an interest-free loan from parent to child in the form of a demand note—that is, an IOU payable on the request of the lender. With the consent of the trustee, the assets being lent are invested in one or more income-producing instruments, and the income generated is taxed at the child's lower rate.

One advantage of the Crown loan arrangement is the ready availability of the assets. If an emergency arises so that you need the money, you have merely to request repayment of the loan; there's no need to wait 10 years and a day, as with the Clifford trust.

The IRS has challenged some crown loan arrangements, contending that they really represent a gift to the child, rather than an interest-free loan. Therefore, you must be certain that the arrangements you establish meet IRS criteria. In particular, make sure that the transaction is clearly labeled a loan, rather than a gift; that the loan is payable on demand; that no provision be made to "forgive" the debt; and that the note specifies that the loan is interest-free. Again, the advice of a knowledgeable attorney is invaluable.

Perhaps the simplest way of obtaining the tax benefits possible under a living trust arrangement is by establishing one or more custodial accounts for your children under the Uniform Gifts to Minors Act (UGMA). It's quite easy to do. First, you get a Social Security number for your child (it can be obtained any time after birth). Then, you transfer money, stocks, bonds, or other assets to the child, to be administered by a custodian for the child's benefit. The custodian can be you or someone else. The assets represent an irrevocable gift to the child and may only be spent on the child's behalf. When the child reaches the age of majority—18 in most states—the assets become his or hers.

Any bank officer or broker will be able to advise you as to the procedures for establishing a UGMA custodial account for your child—or grandchild, for that matter.

A trust arrangement can be a highly effective way of reducing your taxes while providing for the future of your children. However, be sure you understand the legal requirements before you finalize your plans. Otherwise, the tax benefits you'd hoped for may prove illusory.

Wills

• •

Writing a will is one of the most basic—yet most often neglected—steps in financial planning. Here are the essential facts you'll need to know.

By law, you have the right to own property, to use it as you like during your lifetime, and to determine who shall receive it after you die. Everyone makes use of the first two rights on this list, but many fail to exercise their third property right by failing to write a *will*.

A will is simply a set of instructions as to what should be done with your property after you die. It names your heirs, assigns specific shares of your property to each one, and describes any particular conditions under which the distribution should occur. If you fail to prepare a properly executed will, several unpleasant consequences may follow: Your property may not be distributed as you hope it will be; your heirs may suffer a greater tax burden and higher administrative costs; and your family and friends may be subject to needless worry and squabbling. Preparing a will is an essential part of meeting your financial responsibilities.

The instructions you leave in your will are to be carried out by a person you designate as the *executor*. If no one is named in the will as executor, the court will appoint an administrator. The job of executor is an important, sometimes burdensome one. It may include any or all of the following duties:

1. The executor must obtain a copy of the will and submit it to probate—that is, request court approval of its validity.

2. The executor may be required to publish a "notice of death" for a specified period of time.

3. The executor must inventory, appraise, and safeguard all assets of the estate.

4. The executor must open a checking account on behalf of the estate and maintain complete and accurate records of all transactions.

5. The executor must apply for all appropriate death benefits, including those available through life insurance, Social Security, pension plans, the Veterans Administration, labor unions, and fraternal organizations.

6. The executor must pay all outstanding debts of the deceased subject to the statute of limitations.

7. The executor must file and pay local, state, and federal income and estate taxes.

8. The executor must distribute all remaining assets according to the terms of the will.

9. The executor may be required to submit a final accounting to the court.

As you see, it's necessary to choose wisely when naming an executor. It's best to make certain that the person you have in mind is willing to undertake the job and understands what it entails.

Aside from naming the executor, a will should clearly describe how you want your assets distributed after your death. Any knowledgeable lawyer should be able to help you write your will in such a way as to avoid any misleading or unclear statements which could lead to confusion or disputes. Your lawyer will also be able to advise you on particular legal requirements that may apply to your special circumstances and will make sure that your will is properly executed (that is, signed and witnessed in correct legal fashion).

Because personal and family circumstances change, you should review your will at least once every 5 years to make sure that it still reflects your current wishes and needs. If you move to a different state, where different laws apply, you may need to write an entirely new will. If only minor changes are needed from time to time, these can be made by means of a written statement, called a *codicil,* attached to the original document. The help of a lawyer is needed for amending a will too.

As noted in the section "Financial Planning for Women," it is just as important to a wife to have a will as for her husband. A married couple often have *interlocking* or *reciprocal wills* prepared at the same time. These are separate documents carefully interrelated to one another and designed to meet the mutual objectives of both parties. For example, his-and-her wills should specify how the children are to be cared for in the event both parents die at the same time.

Keep your will in a safe place but preferably not in a safe-deposit box; if the box is sealed upon your death, getting into it may be time-consuming and difficult. Rather, have your lawyer keep a copy in his or her files, and keep another copy at home in a place where your family or friends can find it.

What if you die *intestate*—that is, without a will? Your local court will appoint an administrator to distribute your property in accordance with the laws of your state. Outstanding debts and other claims will be paid first; any remaining assets will be distributed to your heirs in proportions determined by state law (and not necessarily to your liking). If no blood relatives can be located, most states will claim ownership of the property.

If you don't want that to happen to your hard-earned wealth, it's easy to avoid: Write a will.

PART THREE

....

A Glossary
of Financial Terms

adjustable-rate mortgage   A type of mortgage in which the interest rate charged may be changed at fixed intervals, usually in response to changes in some predetermined financial index.

alimony   Continuing payments made by one party in a divorce to the other, usually determined by court decree at the time of the settlement. Alimony has traditionally been paid by husbands to wives, although this is no longer invariably the case.

annuity   A form of insurance in which the policyholder, called the *annuitant,* pays a specified sum of money and in return receives regular payments for the rest of his or her life.

appreciation   An increase in the value of any property; used especially in reference to an increase in the value of a stock, bond, or other security.

assay   To analyze gold or silver bullion and so determine the proportion of precious metal it contains.

back-end load   A sales fee or commission charged by the management of a mutual fund at the time the shares in the fund are sold. (See also: *front-end load.*)

balloon mortgage   A type of mortgage in which the entire principal comes due within 2 to 5 years, at which time the loan must be repaid or refinanced at current interest rates.

beneficiary   The person who receives financial benefit as a result of a will, an insurance policy, or a trust fund.

bond   An IOU issued by a corporation or government agency, promising to pay a specified amount of interest for a specified period of time in exchange for an amount of money being lent to the corporation or agency.

broker   A person or firm engaged in buying or selling stocks, bonds, real estate, or other investment instruments on behalf of another. Brokers are normally licensed by one or more government agencies, which monitor and regulate their activities.

bullion   Gold or silver of a specified purity, in the form of coins or, more commonly, bars or ingots.

call   An option giving the right to buy a specified amount of stock at a specified price within a specified time. (See also: *put*.)

callable bond   A bond which may be redeemed at the option of the issuing corporation or government agency before its maturity date.

capital   The total assets of a firm, including cash, land, buildings, equipment, investments, and accounts receivable.

capital gains   Profits from the sale of securities or real estate. If assets are held for longer than 6 months before sale, any profits earned are considered *long-term capital gains* and are eligible for favorable income tax treatment; if the assets are held for 6 months or less, the profits are *short-term capital gains* and are not eligible for such treatment.

cash value   See: *surrender value*.

certificate of deposit   A certificate representing an investment of a specified sum of money in a bank at a specified interest rate guaranteed for a particular period of time.

closing costs   Costs paid by the buyer of a home at the time of purchase. Closing costs include such charges as appraisal and surveying fees, title search costs, lawyers' fees, and so on, and range from 2 percent to as much as 10 percent of the purchase price.

collateral   Property whose value is offered as a guarantee of repayment of a loan. If the loan is not repaid, the creditor is entitled to ownership of the collateral.

commercial bank   A bank which primarily serves business firms, although most commercial banks also accept deposits from and make loans to individuals.

commodity   A basic product bought and sold on a commodity exchange. Examples include wheat, corn, sugar, cotton, soybeans, and minerals such as copper, zinc, gold, and silver.

commodity future   A contract giving the right to buy or sell a specified amount of a certain commodity at a specified price at a specified future time.

common stock A security that represents partial ownership in the issuing corporation. The holder of a share of common stock has the right to receive part of the company's earnings and to vote on certain policy decisions facing the company. (See also: *preferred stock.*)

compound interest Interest computed by applying the percentage rate not only to the principal but to previously made interest payments. The more frequently interest is compounded, the greater the effective yield of an investment.

condominium A form of real estate ownership in which the owner holds the title to his or her own dwelling unit as well as a share in common properties, such as lobbies, parking areas, and recreational facilities.

convertible bond A corporate bond which may be exchanged at the option of the bondholder for shares of common stock in the same corporation.

cooperative A form of real estate ownership in which the owner buys one or more shares in a corporation that owns and manages land and buildings. Each share in the corporation entitles its owner to occupy part of the property, such as an apartment.

coupon bond A bond with interest coupons attached, which are clipped by the holder and redeemed at specified intervals for interest payments.

credit union A savings institution which is owned by its depositors, who are technically considered shareholders. Like a savings bank, a credit union accepts deposits and makes loans, often at lower interest rates than those offered by banks.

creditor A person or institution to which a debt is owed. The holder of a bond issued by a corporation, for example, is a creditor of the corporation.

custodial account A savings or investment account, often in the name of a child, with another person, such as a parent, listed as custodian. The custodian manages the account, but the income belongs to the owner of the account and may normally be used only for his or her benefit.

debenture   A corporate bond whose value is not guaranteed by a pledge of collateral.

depreciation   A decline in the value of a piece of property over time. The depreciation of income-producing property is treated as a loss and so is deductible from income for income tax purposes; the amount of the tax deduction is computed by formulas that vary according to the nature of the property.

diversification   Investment of funds in a variety of instruments having differing yields, maturities, and degrees of risk. Diversification is generally considered a beneficial investment strategy.

dividend   A portion of a company's profits distributed to the stockholders. In a given year, a company's board of directors may or may not pay a dividend, depending on the company's financial status and anticipated future needs.

down payment   A partial payment for a piece of property, such as a home, made at the time of purchase, with the understanding that the balance will be paid later. The size of the down payment required often depends on the creditworthiness of the buyer.

endowment insurance   A form of life insurance in which premium payments are required for a specified period of time, during which the face value of the policy is payable in the event of the death of the policyholder. If the policyholder is still alive at the end of the period, the face value of the policy is paid to him or her in a lump sum.

equity   The value of a piece of property to its owner over and above any portion of that value which has been offered as collateral for a loan. For example, the owner of a house worth $150,000 on which a $90,000 mortgage has been taken has $60,000 in equity.

executor   A person named in a will to manage the settlement of the estate according to the instructions given in the will.

face value   The value of a stock, bond, or insurance policy, usually printed on the front (or "face") of the document. The face value of a security usually differs from its selling price.

Federal Reserve   The central monetary authority of the United States. The Federal Reserve issues currency, sells U.S. government securities, and extends credit to member banks.

foreclosure   The process whereby the holder of a mortgage receives ownership of the property after the owner has failed to repay the loan.

front-end load   A sales fee or commission charged by the management of a mutual fund at the time the shares in the fund are purchased. (See also: *back-end load*.)

income averaging   A method of computing income tax liability by which an unusually large amount of income received in a single year is spread out over several years, thus reducing the rate of taxation.

individual retirement account (IRA)   A savings or investment plan which allows an individual to accumulate funds toward retirement while deferring income taxes on both the amount invested and the interest earned.

inflation   An increase in the general level of prices for goods and services in an economy.

insurance   A contract in which one party—usually a company organized for the purpose—promises to pay a specified sum of money in the event that the second party suffers a financial loss through death, accident, injury, or other misfortune.

intestacy   The condition of dying without having made a valid will. When a person dies intestate, his or her estate is usually distributed in accordance with state laws.

junk bond   A corporate bond rated BB or lower by Standard and Poor's rating service or Ba or lower by Moody's rating service. Junk bonds carry a relatively high degree of risk, but pay a high rate of return as well.

Keogh plan   A savings or investment plan for self-employed persons whose purpose and benefits resemble those of the IRA. However, the Keogh plan allows a larger amount of money to be sheltered from income taxes each year.

limited-payment life insurance   A type of life insurance in which premium payments are made only for a specified period of time, such as 20 years. The face value of the policy is paid on the death of the policyholder, no matter when it occurs.

liquidity   The ease with which invested funds can be sold or otherwise converted into cash.

living trust   A trust which takes effect during the lifetime of the person who establishes it.

load   The commission charged by the firm that manages a mutual fund; normally a percentage of the amount invested.

margin   Cash or credit advanced by a broker to allow the purchase of stocks or bonds for only a fraction of the full price. Making such a purchase is known as *buying on margin*.

maturity   The date on which a loan must be paid, or the period during which the loan may remain outstanding.

money market   The market in which various kinds of high-yielding, short-term securities are bought and sold. Interest rates on the money market respond quickly to changes in financial and economic conditions.

money market deposit account   A bank account whose funds are invested in money market securities.

money market fund   A mutual fund which invests in money market securities.

mortgage   A loan made with the ownership of personal property, such as a house, given as collateral. If the loan is not repaid, the holder of the mortgage has a right to ownership of the property.

municipal bond   A bond issued by a state or local government or one of its agencies. Interest earned on municipal bonds is normally exempt from federal income tax, and sometimes from state and local income taxes as well.

mutual fund   An investment company that pools the funds of many individuals and invests them in stocks, bonds, or other securities. Those who invest through a mutual fund are called *shareholders* and receive dividends whose size depends on the performance of the fund's investments.

no-load fund   A mutual fund that does not charge a commission on investments.

option   A contract giving the right to buy or sell a specified quantity of stock at a specified price within a specified period of time.

par value   The value printed on the face of a stock or bond; often the same as the initial selling price. The resale price of a stock or bond usually differs from the par value.

penny stock   Any stock selling for a low price per share, usually one dollar or less. Penny stocks are usually considered speculative investments.

pension   An arrangement in which regular payments are made to a retired employee by his or her former employer or by a government agency.

points   An interest charge levied by a mortgage lender at the time a house is sold. For each point charged, the buyer must pay the lending institution 1 percent of the mortgage amount. On some mortgages, no points are charged; on others, 3 points, 5 points, or more.

portfolio   The complete array of investment holdings belonging to an individual or an institution.

preferred stock   A security representing partial ownership in the issuing corporation. Holders of preferred stock have a prior claim to the earnings and assets of the company over holders of common stock. Preferred stock usually carries no stockholder voting privileges and usually pays a pre-fixed annual dividend.

premium   (1) The amount of money paid to purchase a life insurance policy or an annuity. (2) The amount by which the selling price of a stock or bond exceeds its face value or par value.

principal   An amount of money lent or invested.

prospectus   A formal document prepared by a corporation issuing stocks, bonds, or other securities, which is made available to all prospective buyers of the securities. The prospectus must include certain facts about the company and the security as specified by the Securities and Exchange Commission, including the names of the corporation's officers, its financial condition, and its recent record of profits and losses.

put   An option giving the right to sell a specified amount of stock at a specified price within a specified time. (See also: *call*.)

redemption   The repurchase of a bond or other form of indebtedness by the issuing corporation or government agency.

registered bond   A bond registered in its owner's name. Interest is paid at regular intervals to the registered owner; the bond may be transferred only by changing the registration.

reinvestment   (1) The practice of returning all or some of a company's profits to the business for use in financing growth, plant or equipment purchases, and so on. (2) An arrangement whereby dividends or interest earned by shares in a mutual fund is automatically used to purchase additional shares in the fund.

return on investment   The amount of profit received on an investment as a percentage of the amount of capital invested. Also called *yield*.

savings bank   A state-chartered financial institution which accepts deposits and offers loans at regulated interest rates.

savings and loan association   A financial institution, technically owned by depositors, which invests primarily in home mortgages.

Securities and Exchange Commission (SEC)   The U.S. federal regulatory agency charged with controlling the issuing, buying, and selling of stocks, bonds, and other securities. The SEC supervises the operation of securities exchanges, registers brokers, and enforces laws governing the issuance of securities.

security   A written instrument that either certifies partial ownership of a business or promises repayment of a debt by a business or government agency.

shareholder   (1) The owner of one or more shares of stock in a corporation. (2) The owner of one of more shares in a mutual fund.

speculation   Buying stocks or other investments in the hope of reselling them at a large profit relatively quickly. Speculative investments generally offer higher growth potential than other investments, but carry a correspondingly greater degree of risk.

stock   A share in the ownership of a corporation.

stock split   The division of the outstanding shares of a corporation's stock into a larger number of shares. A stock split results in each shareholder owning more shares of stock, each with a lower value than that of the original shares.

stock warrant   A certificate giving the right to buy a specified number of shares of stock at a specified price within a specified period of time. Warrants are often attached to bonds or to certificates of preferred stock; in some cases, they may be bought and sold separately as investments in their own right.

surrender value   The amount of money for which a life insurance policy may be cashed in prior to the death of the policyholder. The surrender value of a policy usually increases annually during the life of the policy. Also called *cash value*.

tax bracket   The level at which an individual's income is taxed, normally determined by the size of his or her taxable income. The higher the taxable income, the higher the tax bracket and the higher the rate of taxation.

tax-deferred   Not subject to income tax until a later date.

tax-exempt   Not subject to income tax.

tax shelter   Any device or strategy by which a taxpayer can avoid paying income taxes on a portion of his or her income. Examples include individual retirement accounts (IRAs), Keogh plan accounts, 401(k) accounts, and oil and gas shelters.

term   The period of time during which an investment or an insurance policy is in effect.

term insurance   A form of life insurance in which the benefit is payable only if the insured person dies during a specified period.

testamentary trust   A trust which takes effect only after the death of the person who established it.

Treasury bill   A short-term obligation of the federal government, sold in minimum amounts of $10,000 with maturity periods of 3, 6, and 12 months. Treasury bills are sold at a discount from their face value; the discount represents prepayment of the interest on the loan. At maturity, the bill is redeemable for its full face value.

Treasury bond   A long-term obligation of the federal government, sold in minimum amounts of $1000 or $5000 (depending on maturity) with maturity periods of 10 to 30 years. Treasury bonds are sold both by the federal government and in the secondary market, where their prices fluctuate in accordance with changes in interest rates.

Treasury note   An intermediate-term obligation of the federal government, sold in minimum amounts of $1000 with maturity periods of 1 to 10 years. Like Treasury bonds, Treasury notes are available on the secondary market at varying prices.

trust   An arrangement whereby property is transferred from one party, called the *grantor,* to a second party, called the *trustee,* for the benefit of a third party, called the *beneficiary.* Trusts are usually established in order to reduce tax liability, streamline the transfer of assets after death, or maintain some control over the use of assets after they have been transferred.

unit trust An investment plan in which an investor buys a share in a portfolio of corporate or municipal bonds. The investor receives a specified rate of interest on his or her investment payable over a specified period of time, depending on the maturity dates of the bonds in the portfolio.

universal life insurance A type of life insurance policy in which part of the premium payment is used to provide life insurance protection and the remainder is invested in any of a variety of high-yielding instruments.

utility A private industry which has been given the status of a state-regulated monopoly by a local or national government. In most parts of the United States, the corporations providing electricity, gas, telephone service, water, and mass transportation are run as utilities. Utility stocks are usually considered safe but relatively low-yielding investments.

volume (1) The number of shares of a particular stock that is bought or sold on a given day. (2) The total number of shares of stock that is bought or sold on an organized exchange on a given day.

whole life insurance A type of life insurance policy in which premium payments are continued at the same level throughout the life of the policyholder, with death benefits payable whenever the policyholder dies.

will A written document prepared according to legal specifications which provides for distribution of the writer's assets after his or her death.

yield See *return on investment.*

zero coupon bond   A corporate, municipal, or Treasury bond sold at a discount from its face value. Upon maturity, the zero coupon bond is redeemed for the full face value, with the discount representing the interest earned on the investment.

Catalog

If you are interested in a list of fine Paperback
books, covering a wide range of subjects
and interests, send your name and address,
requesting your free catalog, to:

McGraw-Hill Paperbacks
1221 Avenue of Americas
New York, N.Y. 10020